Sesh Sukhdeo

Unlock the Collaboration Code

Enhancing Personal and Business Growth

Createspace 2018

ISBN 978-1-5136-2469-3

Table of Contents

"When we start the journey of collaboration, the ultimate goal is to achieve something more valuable than we can individually".

Sesh Sukhdeo

Endorsements

"Sesh Sukhdeo has made a significant contribution that is worthy of our attention. His perspective and solutions will inspire you; his guidance is insightful and trustworthy."

—Robert Porter Lynch, CEO of The Warren Company Inc. www.warrenco.com

"This book will help to spread the concept and practice of supply chain collaboration, and its associated benefits."

—Professor Tom Cherrett, University of Southampton and Julian Allen, University of Westminster (both leading research projects into supply chain collaboration)

"Sesh is absolutely second to none when it comes to fostering truly collaborative relationships. He creates space to explore shared areas of interest for innovation. His unusually open sharing style provides value to any business engaging with him. I have not met anyone quite like him."

—Alex Blakemore, CEO.

"If there is anyone who can unlock value, innovate and create paradigm shifts, it's Sesh. A real enjoy collaborating with."

—Michael Boulton, Strategic Development Director Whistl. www.whistl.co.uk

"Sesh understands the art of Influence: he leaves his mark on everything he does. Having worked with Sesh over the years, I have seen people's lives from all walks, careers, sectors and age groups transform from the value he creates. Sesh's insights highlight that Organizations don't collaborate – it's people who collaborate. A Great read for everyone involved in value creation."

—Dr. Grace Ngungi-Karanja, Partnership Specialist at USAID Kenya Youth Employment and Skills Program

"It is rare in modern business to find someone who cares about networking as much as Sesh. In this age of technological development, there is a serious need for innovators who can blend traditional business with new technology: this collaboration is vital and what Sesh highlights skillfully in this book."

—Nathan Kelleher, Vice President of Global Carrier Strategy Neopost Shipping.www.temando.co.uk

About the Author

Over the course of his career, Sesh Sukhdeo has assembled countless engagements and collaborative projects within the public and private sector globally. There is little that Mr. Sukhdeo has not understood when it comes to dealing with those thorniest problems we face; he is regarded by his peer group as an expert in driving growth through collaborative engagement, not as intriguing theories, but as a hands-on practitioner.

He does not waste time; with his innovative thinking and specialized methodology. He quickly creates synergies between and within organizations, the results of which have impressed and delighted thousands. He understands the kinetics that underpins the process of building relationships and how influence impacts personal and corporate growth.

Seeing beyond the horizon, Sesh quickly guides others towards the value that they miss. His intentions are directed towards everything which influences success. Subtlety outlining where efforts are lacking and what needs to be done to make a difference.

Sesh can help overcome those barriers to cooperation when others cannot. He believes that the solution lies in the balance of motivation and state of mind. Obviously, motivations are different for everyone. Therefore, it is essential to find a common thread that resonates for all involved. This is Sesh Sukhdeo's area of expertise.

During his career, Sesh has come to realize that many individuals have simply never realized the benefits of cooperative problem-solving and the value of genuine collaboration. Rather than working in tandem with others, they find themselves having to overcome unnecessary obstacles alone. They operate within rigid hierarchies that stall their progress and reduce their creative inspirations which lock them into a state of flux.

Introduction

This book is a result of the wonderful feedback received from the delegates who attended the United Nations Junior Chamber of Commerce, New York Partnership Summit, where I spoke about the importance of collaboration, synergy, and entrepreneurship. I showcased how collaborative development is spearheading economic and social growth, and outlined the enablers required to make a difference.

I drew reference to the fact that Collaboration and Cooperation have become such popular terms, and that every meeting we seem to all attend seems to be spiced up with promises of extended value, opportunities to partner and a call for greater synergy. Global Leaders and influential groups agreed likewise, we shared the importance of breaking down barriers which drive interactions, goodwill and intentions forward. What we do know is that no one walks around with a name tag proclaiming, "Hi, I'm a collaborative leader, follow me." Instead, we see people at all levels make a difference, resulting in enhanced communication and momentum.

One of the greatest challenges facing leadership is identifying those initiatives that are worth backing, and those individuals best suited to drive efforts and dialogue forward, and thinking about the myriad of barriers which could get in the way.

What we know is that job titles alone do not always guarantee success, many simply live on their titles and demonstrate varying degrees of goodwill and collaborative ethos, but, when you come across those who resonate and want to make a difference, you know it, feel it and want to be part of it. At the same time, it is worth reflecting on those who sit idle and place little value on sharing, preferring to encourage competitive or mischievous efforts rather than cooperative engagement.

As a disruptive business coach, Investor and strategic advisor, I have spent countless hours engaging with senior executives, teams and people of influence across a wide range of endeavors, what I find striking is that corporations are waking up to the fact that change and disruption, are inevitable, imminent, and omnipresent. The new leaders of the world, will leave their mark for future generations and accept that collaboration plays a strong influence on people's lives, careers and the organizations they represent.

My objective is to put forward relevant and thought provoking frames of reference which will make a difference, to our individual roles, team efforts, and those external venture creation activities such as joint ventures, strategic alliances, formal partnerships, outsourcing relationships, and virtually all other types of business-to-business or public-to-private sector formal /informal relationships.

In the following pages, I explore both the driving and restraining forces that demand our consideration. I begin by describing the way collaboration fits into modern businesses and organizations. Then I drill down into the issues that commonly arise in these spaces. After that, I showcase the traits of an effective collaborator and provide a range of guidelines to help navigate a successful way forward. I have taken this approach because if we are to confront the challenges of the future effectively, we must identify those areas that need to be advanced and improved. To achieve these lofty and necessary ends, we must learn how to establish the mechanisms that let us reach a consensus, and in due course, achieve a successful conclusion.

As civic, consumer, business and governments change, some of our own habits and tendencies which have stagnated will need to be enhanced if we are to stay relevant and current. We cannot sit still, or view the new world with old eyes and old methods if we are to chart fresh waters. Despite modern globalization creating a market that stretches across the whole world, some businesses can act a lot like countries, with borders and checkpoints riddled with no end of bureaucracy and no end in sight. The experience is frustrating for those involved and can leave everyone feeling bewildered.

I set forth the importance of Collaboration as the answer to many of today's most pressing personal, business, social, and political challenges. In the following chapters, I will highlight its benefits and considerations with respect to its role and influence on transformation.

I present real examples of businesses and people from around the globe to illustrate the depth of how collaboration crisscrosses their daily paths and is embedded in ethos and practice.

Like a skilled locksmith, the effective collaborator knows that every lock requires a different key and combination to open. When the key is damaged, it is almost impossible to open; when plans don't go as expected, there is a tendency to force a way forward, and in doing so, we place undue pressure, which results in the key snapping. When this happens, we search for a specialist to resolve the crisis at hand. I have spent much of my working life as that locksmith, using a variety of tools and techniques to open the doors to authentic opportunities and solving problems in the process.

In my experience and those highlighted, it clearly shows that collaboration when executed well produces faster growth and helps us to be better positioned when adversity strikes. By building truly effective trust-based relationships we also instinctively share knowledge and open mutually beneficial social, economic (and indeed, political) dialogue. The exchange results in the liberation of new ideas and possibilities.

Despite the benefits of collaborations, many individuals and businesses remain wary of entering extended relationships, — understandably, to say the least. Almost all of us have heard horror stories of relationship, and business collaborations that went disastrously wrong, even when the potential results would have been beneficial to all parties. Perhaps the most common example of when collaboration stalls are when there is a breakdown of trust between different parties, or where personality differences bring a halt to synergy development as ego's trump goodwill.

Another disheartening situation is when I watch startups explode into the market only to fall apart because its teams could not resolve internal differences and misunderstanding creep overturns progress. How often do we see those headlines about business or management relationships breaking down, misunderstandings taking hold and the clunkiness of inherent bureaucracy knocking progress backward?

In business or corporate offices, NGOs, and governments around the world, we hear terms like collaboration, partnering, and value maximization so frequently that they have become mainstream; it seems as if they have been around forever, and that everyone embraces it. We know this is not true, if this was the case, we would not hear about the scrupulous working practices or see win-lose mindsets at work, or see headline news of corporate partnership fallouts, or see Public-Private partnerships falter.

In the spirit of collaboration, much of this text is substantiated with the words of my colleagues, mentors, business partners, and global thought leaders, for example, Robert Porter Lynch, a global leadership influencer. I was trained by Robert some twenty years ago in the US, and it's a pleasure to engage and work alongside him still today.

He wrote the famous chapter "Fostering Champions" for Peter Drucker's book, The Leader of the Future (Jossey-Bass, 1997). Robert provides an important insight in one of his strategic alerts: "Creating an Age of Re-Enlightenment & Collaborative Excellence," which outlines that we live in a chaotic, confusing time, filled with a muddled, mongrelized view of culture, leadership, the human race's relationship to itself, as well as its institutions, economy, businesses, and environment. Our world is searching for solutions— and not finding them. Our people are distrustful and anxiety-ridden. Our economies are not prospering. According to the strategic alert, employees are disengaged.

He outlines that our economic systems are under attack. Our political and civil institutions are profoundly distrusted, and often dysfunctional. Robert's insights corroborate the need to search for alternate frames of reference and activities that drive better outcomes. He stated, "We require a sea change shift in leadership and culture. New thinking, new ideas, inspirations, and models are in order".

What I also find inspirational is the following comment from Robert's article, "The Stirring Call for a Re-Enlightenment," It states, "The 21st century must embrace its predecessor's values, while also enjoining basic responsibilities every human has to each other, their community, and to their environment".

Building on the above, collaboration impacts social and economic development in several ways. It allows us to spread and receive knowledge, it fosters creativity and dramatically alters the way in which we conduct business, and engage with others. Shifting one's creative labor from "for themselves and by themselves" to "for the team and by the team" changes the shape of not just our businesses but our political and social landscapes. The process of collaborating well can yield a range of experiences; when done correctly, it can leave you and those around you feeling empowered, inspired, and engaged.

Many leaders acknowledge and cite the importance of collaboration. I recently met the chairman of a global group and, in passing, I asked for his view on collaboration and its importance within a business. His response was very fitting, "I certainly agree that collaboration will be a critical requirement for companies moving forward into a much more complex and fast-changing world."—John Neill, Chairman & CBE of the Unipart Group.

Developing a practical approach to collaboration starts with a positive mindset and a solid understanding of what you are trying to achieve. The incessant image of the finish line, whatever that looks like to you, provides an end goal and intended outcome. When you can truly visualize it, and understand it, it becomes easier to reach. However, if your comprehension of collaboration is vague, intentions will be weak and efforts will falter.

Consider the range of questions

- What is the biggest problem you need to solve and could collaboration influence it?

- Are you able to achieve growth on your own, or do you need to work with others?

- Do you need to break new boundaries, or seeking collaboration to co-create new service offerings, if so, how will you achieve this?

When we think of collaboration, we also need to look at who, not just why we need to collaborate. When you do, you will establish that there are three distinct stakeholders: you, the organization, and the broader group in which you operate. A collaborative person will unlock value, they will tease open snippets of ideas, and will value the differences which exist. The organization, will set the tone and systems in place to innovate, reward and deliver, it creates the ecosystem in which you operate and will reflect the tensions/elasticity through which ideas flow. The wider group is where value exchanges cross different boundaries from one department, or business to another.

While there are many elements which contribute towards success, to me, one of the many worthy of mention is the value of conversation, and the resulting insights which can flow, done well, it is meaningful, when shallow and false we find egos rising which trump all those efforts of merit. I make this point because engagement is not always straightforward, it can be riddled with issues, miss understandings, and petty infighting.

In the following chapters, I have considered these things, and have devised a range of approaches and solutions to guide us along a path to greater success. So, let us investigate these challenges together so that we deliver prosperity and delight for you and those around you. I believe that each one of us has a vast potential to make a difference, to feel great and provide awesome value.

Are you ready?

Chapter 1: Preparing For Change

The future is rushing towards us at a rate of knots: social inclusion, business diversity, science and innovation at all levels continues to grow in quantum, so many influences cut across our daily lives, we are seeing glimpses of emerging technologies dramatically shifting market dynamics with just one release, as such, we need to ensure we are prepared for the change that's about to come. We are about to experience several paradigm shifts as the power of technology manifests new services and potential. We may indeed see existing business models becoming obsolete in a few years to come if they don't transform, diversify or innovate. Think of those substantial brands who have vanished because they and their boards failed to anticipate and understand the changes which were taking place on their watch.

Some leaders continue, day in and out, hour after hour, as if they have some form of secret code to access the future, and the minds of others, when in fact, they don't. They speculate with commands, set strategic visions hoping that everyone will follow, and nothing happens. When people are partially present in mind, and commitment stalls, efforts nose dive south, and progress stalls.

New and established organizations will experience change; some will try to gain an advantage on their own, while others will come together to jointly innovative with elements of their value and supply chain. As we enhance our understanding of science, and computing power rises, such as sophisticated Artificial Intelligence (AI) and Machine learning, we will break new boundaries, forcing the need to innovate and adapt, I foresee the need for greater collaborative engagement to increase so that we keep up with the pace of change. A decade ago, there was a tremendous amount of investment taking place in robotics, drones and the autonomous vehicle sector; today these innovations are visible on production lines. Imagine chatbots which engage with us and drones which can clean solar panels, such is the change which is on the way.

How is your business and how are you innovating as you move forward?

These changes give rise to a different future, and if we are not prepared to meet these challenges, we will be swept aside. I also foresee the emergence of new environmental and social strategies, which will go far beyond the usual doctrines of corporate responsibility. I'm not alone: Arif Naqvi, CEO of the Abraaj Group, a leading Private Equity Group, has also said this: in a news piece carried by Reuters. "If you want to be a great company in the 21st century, you first have to be a good company that realizes it must benefit its communities." If we are correct in this assessment, then we need to prepare for this change by asking how we, as individuals, can influence these changes to our mutual benefit. Mr. Naqvi sets the strategic mission of his firm based on his desire to make a difference.

"In the investment firm I founded, we gauge and manage the prospects of our global investments against Sustainable Development Goals metrics. The opportunities they outline are unprecedented, with this one pre-condition. If you want to be a great company in the 21st century, you first have to be a good company that realizes it must benefit its communities. Mr. Naqvi's position has influenced its mission and underpins its overall strategic direction. The company is built on its broader impact, which permeates its investment decisions.

The questions which need addressing are:

- How do we address those dramatic shifts in knowledge, understanding, and experiences that we are about to face?

- How do we incubate new ideas to innovative mutually beneficial interaction?

The answer is either we do it alone or collaborate, where we combine efforts to yield additional value. This is (or at least, it should be) defined as a win-win arrangement, it is mutually beneficial and reflects a commitment and efforts to achieve something better. We need to recognize and accept that we can't do everything on our own, so we must learn to take advantage of the benefits that are available through the involvement and inclusion of others.

It is only through experience that we see wisdom prevail. Over the years, I have learned not to celebrate success only because the ideas seem right to me, or because meetings start well. It is stronger when commitments are made. I have seen game-changing ideas dismissed through the ambush of others' ego, and seen trust disabled because of the lack of integrity, in fact, my list can go on for pages; my point is that all too often talk and intentions come to nothing, great ideas are quietly abandoned, or just wither away without anyone even taking notice that they have disappeared. One of the reasons for this occurring is that not everyone understands what value is, much less how to unlock it.

Taking this into account, how do we embrace the various value systems of all participating parties?

Firstly, we should not dismiss those who are silent and different or commit to growth purely as a paper exercise. Achieving laudable success and growth is going to require reflection and new efforts. Perhaps the most important adaptation is to leverage the intelligence and resourcefulness of the minds within our ecosystems. Observe, rather than demand, and guide rather than push. Imagine being in a forest with a group of your peers, and you hold the map. You are not an expert in climbing or survival, but you must lead because you have the map. To lead your group out, towards the objective, you have the necessary directions: you all must go South, you guide others to a path, but you seek insights from your team, to ensure your way forward is not futile.

Leaders that are domineering and overbearing, intimidating those beneath them into accepting their recommendations as the best possible outcome will run entirely against the grain, it is destructive and can lead the group to be lost or confused. There is merit on the strength of the collaborative mindset, areas of contentions can be quickly resolved and a reduction to change can occur. I infer that trust, rather than competition, will become a critical factor in our development and we need to embrace the importance of collaborative leadership and understand its influence on ours and everyone's success.

You cannot collaborate by just reading a book; you must actively engage in the process. Unquestionably, the greater the number of perspectives assessed, the more likely we are to eliminate those blind spots which cloud our thinking and in turn reduce if not eliminate the mistakes we make due to shallow thinking or false perceptions.

What I am getting at is that the central issue here is of Influence. Who is influencing whom and just how much influence is being exerted? You can't answer this until you drill down and understand the dimensions of intrinsic and extrinsic influence.

I have described four influence levers which affect us all.

Four leverage points:

1. Growth: Those opportunities with strategic importance, to you, within you and external.

2. Risk: Reduction: Including prioritization and evaluation.

3. Value chain: Unlock, create, and enhance the current ecosystem.

4. Structural capabilities: Sustainable competitive efforts and advantage/agility.

Each of the above levers impacts success.

To create powerful paradigm shifts we need to reframe some of our thoughts, especially those which hinder and limit dialogue. I suggest that an open mind will extract far higher value, than a closed mind, we know through history that ignorance often besets us with further challenges and issues which no amount of money can fix, the consequences are so far reaching that they can consume us for decades.

We will need to adapt, indeed work with others to co-create the answer and solution. To think otherwise is simply foolish. How then could collaboration impact or influence your current position and company?

Collaboration and cooperation obviously make this process much easier, it provides an impetus on shared research and development, and for co-leadership to work together to solve inherent issues across all sectors, government, businesses and corporate entities of every size, structure, and geographic locations. We have seen entire countries re-modeling their current value systems to be more socially inclusive, in doing so they set new tones for future generations and open new channels of dialogue and activate those levers earlier described.

Elements of successful collaboration include:

- Clearly defining and agreeing on the roles of stakeholders/partners in the collaborative process.

- Open communication within teams to share the information necessary to carry out tasks.

- Consensus about goals and the methods for completing projects or tasks.

- Recognition and respect for the contribution of all collaborators.

- Identifying obstacles and addressing problems cooperatively as they occur.

- Placing group goals above personal satisfaction and/or recognition.

- Willingness to apologize for any missteps you make and forgive others for genuine mistakes.

- Allowing those involved to contribute and drive change.

- A recognition that a value exchange will take place, and it can come from anywhere and anyone.

So, what's your leverage point?

Chapter 2: Strategic Insights

There are times when we confuse some of our greatest thoughts with irrelevance and struggle to understand what is needed to win the battle and get to the finish line. We will never move forward if all we do is go over the past like a scratched record, if we do, all we are doing is simply replaying the same old, repeatedly. What will strike a chord is an inspirational dialogue which solves those inherent issues and problems.

When we ignore fact and place ourselves in low self-esteem, our ideas will become bogged down, and we will experience moments of confusion. What's worst is trying to operate with a constant barrage of negative thought. Listen to the conversations around you, how many of them reflect issues with people, ethics, behavior, wrong doing, or those unnecessary barriers placed which stalls progress and instill backwardness? No battle can be won in such rhetoric. What is needed is an uplifting mindset.

Whatever the situation you are reacting to, it is important to remain relaxed and calm. My strong recommendation is to respond, and not to overreact. If someone criticizes you, whether it is justified or not, take the criticism with good grace. If their critique was demeaning and condescending, do not respond in the same manner. Learn to shrug off insults as though they never happened. Those who see your calm demeanor and unflinching nature will respect you and may be inspired to do the same.

Some people find it easy to grasp the context and recognize ideas of merit, which are strategic, and make a difference, in doing so, they help to counter those opposing forces which get in the way. Taking a moment to reflect, have you had a remarkable moment of serendipity, from where a brilliant idea emerged, at first it seems to appear by luck or chance, yet, it leaves you feeling inspired and eager to follow? If so, what was special about the moment? Was it that the idea was powerful and it stood out amongst all the other ideas?

At a recent senior executive roundtable, I was asked to share some insights into the following: "How do we best place our efforts to shift thinking and our direction"? I suggested that an essential first step is to break down the barriers which confine ones thinking and understanding, I outlined four components which I felt were worthy of mention.

These pillars are held together by strong intents; a weak intention will negatively impact progress; a meaningful well intended purpose will power up our probabilities of success and stabilizes how and where we wish to place our efforts.

These pillars are the vision pillar, strategy pillar, execution pillar, and the metrics pillar.

As you review each of them below– consider how they relate to you?

1. Vision: The way in which you communicate shared views of the future. It is how you describe the success which is to come.

2. Strategy: Represents the tactics and decisions which need to be made to achieve your vision.

3. Execution: Characterized by how efficiently you carry out your plans and intentions.

4. Metrics: What you measure and the values you place against them.

The value of developing strategic insights cascades to everyone who is involved in supporting and creating a value exchange, it requires engagement, and a resulting experience, it should be frictionless as possible, void of ego and one up man ship.

What we do know is that there will be similarities between the problems we face and that previous solutions are guideposts for our subsequent efforts. When weak intentions are present progress will slip away; a strong purpose breaks new boundaries and creates a chain reaction when you combine insight with intuition it is truly kinetic and has a force which generates momentum.

We also experience those gut feeling moment, which is where our unconscious reasoning propels us forward to do something without telling us why or how. We don't truly understand why those Intuitive waves of expression exist, but, what I can say is that is so powerful that it has inspired centuries' worth of research and inquiry across significant strands of knowledge relating to purpose, the mind, philosophy and psychology.

Over time, I have accepted that intuition is different to thinking and thoughts. It seems to flow from somewhere other than my head. We can connect with intuition, but we struggle to pay attention to it and are unable to hear its calling. When we learn how to tune into our emotions, you will better observe and listen, which is critical to collaborative engagement.

Before heading full throttle into your growth plan, the following questions are worthy of consideration.

-.Has collaboration driven growth for you so far, if so what were the results?

- What are you hoping to achieve by collaborating?

- How important is it and what sort of decisions are needed to move forward?

- What are the stumbling blocks envisaged and how will they be resolved?

- Do you have the right team members involved, and can they influence progress?

- Will there be measurable benefits?

- Will collaboration affect your career and success?

- Will collaborative working 'add value' to you, your team and the broader organization, i.e., will it justify the time and effort?

- Do you risk 'mission drift' away from core activities by collaborating?

Organizations which are seeking greater innovation, cooperation, and creativity will find the time to foster the flow of goodwill amongst others – when leaders fail to lubricate the efforts of progress, friction and fractures appear in progress. Egos will take hold and trump all worthy intents. When this occurs, it leaves us feeling as if are crawling to the finish line.

The secret to achieving paradigm shifts which elevate progress is to allow people no matter where and who they are in the organization to be part of the overall journey. I have come across countless examples of leaders trying to solve challenging problems on their own, which could have been solved sooner if they tapped into the vault of good will which exists, all that was required was the concept of inclusive engagment.

The following list will help re-energize the collective focus and help drive progress forward.

- Ensure that the people on the team are encouraged, and know that their work will make a difference.

- Allow people to seize the moment and not get bogged down or sidetracked.

- When the team is faced with bottlenecks or mental blocks, debate and discuss.

I have found that all too often, people and firms jump into relationships without considering their structure and organizing principles, in such a case, it is difficult to construct consistent efforts which build momentum. We must find ways to tap into the reservoir of internal wisdom we possess.

When you take the time to review the environments we tend to work in, they seem to fit what I describe as either an open or closed system settings. The closed system works within strict, codified boundaries. Discussions confined to a selected few or a specific department, acting as a sort of incubator for internal dialogue. The open system is fluid, allowing people from all departments to contribute through interaction at will. Whether you are working with an open or closed group, the challenges faced will be different; nonetheless, it is possible to inspire new possibilities when we engage in the right way. If you look at your existing work environment or team setting, are you operating in a closed or open system?

It's worth noting that one type of system does not necessarily trump another. Open is not always better than closed, what does matter is the character of the leader and the tactics used to achieve the results.

I am frequently asked, 'Does a formalized group have any benefit over an informal one? What I have found is that formalized groups often experience greater personality conflicts as power, politics and the need to win exists, whereas the informal group may lose its sense of direction if not held together. There is no right or wrong answer! Between these two extremes lies the point that I refer to as the "Promise of Potential," that place where all things are possible, where improvement, innovation, and enhanced capabilities thrive.

We have varying degrees of understanding, and differences in our unique personalities, some are expressive, and others are simply an undertone, and hardly noticed. There are also those who are genuine, and there are those who are simply put deceptive with rancor, and hell-bent on derailing anything you do, in pursuit of their own glory. The later causes friction and derails the will to make a positive difference.

There have been times when I set my stall to collaborate yet those in the team are geared up to commemorate! Wanting to derail, sidetrack and create havoc so that genuine progress falters. I am not alone in this experience, all you have to do is assess why some teams don't perform as well as they should, and you will begin to see that it boils down to skill, experience, and mindset. I have gotten used to this, and see beyond such naivety. Thinking about it, there are few organizations where some form of drama or another is not taking place, or where discontent does not exist. When I come across such situations, I don't respond like a raging bull; instead, my armory of wisdom counters such efforts, and I refuse to give up or feel defeated.

Critical to progress is the notion that when we gently steer conversations along constructive lines, even when frustrations exist, or tensions rise, the opportunity to lay down the spirit to resolve exists. Do not enter discussions or negotiations without due care and attention. We have all experienced moments of knowing that a conversation lacks merit, and that some people are not truthful, in such cases, the ability to carefully navigate such choppy waters is needed.

Many people around you wish to add value, not because of their job titles, but, the desire to simply make a difference, there DNA is set to be good, honest and they genuinely want to make a difference, they care. These individuals will arrive without calling, and unless we are alert they will slip past us, like the chain of a bike, they provide momentum and drive a new kinetic force which keeps you moving forward.

Take the self-test and see if you master the qualities required to collaborate:

- Are you adept at building honest, open personal relationships?

- Can you establish a bond of trust with and among others?

- Will you be able to embrace the diversity of thoughts and experiences if it helps you achieve your goals?

- Is it possible to let go of the belief that you have all the answers?

- Do you agree that it is essential to ask the right questions at the right time?

- Can you listen to others with an open mind?

- Can you abide by your commitments?

- Can you resolve conflicts with and among others?

- Do you feel it is crucial to reach decisions by consensus?

- Are there people around you who truly make a difference?

The more of the above you do, the stronger your ability will be to embrace collaboration.

I often refer to synergy because it is so critical to progress, it is what underpins collaboration. Not only does our thinking need to be connected, so does our efforts in our respective ecosystems we operate in. To gain a glimpse how synergy transcends across people to our physical workspace. Think about the growth of co-shared work offices, which resonate openness, spaces where we can have casual conversations and incidental catch ups. Huddle zones for team building inspire greater connections and are a buzzing hive of activities.

There are some brilliant examples of co-shared workspace design. If you are interested, then visit www.huckletree.com - which seems to have made its mark, it's one of London's fastest growing co-working communities supporting a diverse mix of entrepreneurs, startups, and bigger businesses.

The idea behind co workspace is that greater interactions take place, and that cooperative groups reach out beyond the narrow confines of one office, one meeting room, and even one organization to encompass those whom we would not usually engage with. It is designed to allow diversity of thought to be expressed beyond the norm. Striving for anything less leads to restrictive thinking and siloed innovation and an atmosphere which is dull and void. The benefits of a co-shared workspace are that like-minded people, with similar goals, can come together to share, explore and collaborate, to get things done.

Beyond the walls of an organization is a far greater and dynamic ecosystem, where collaboration across the value chain impacts people's lives. Some run parallel to global developmental agendas. It was a great pleasure to learn about the vision and mission of a leading entrepreneur, Pramod Saxena, Founder and Chairman of Oxigen, a FinTech company, a true game changer. Although its operations are substantial in India, its ability to support emerging markets through collaborative channel strategies would bring about an immediate solution to some of the issues of other unbanked citizens around the globe. Interestingly, The United Nations refers to this as part of their social and financial inclusion goals.

Oxigen Services is a leader in the digital payments and FinTech landscape. The company's services impact inclusion in its true sense. Oxigen transforms lives by providing access to banking and financial services on a mature, trusted network. A closer look at this business reveals a true success story, with the potential to be one of those megabrands which serve the under-deserved.

They are set to create one of India's largest financial infrastructure, which empowers the last-mile ecosystem to enable and support financial services for the population, driving the country from a cash-based to a cashless economy, as part of a national collaborative platform. Even US leading economists are calling the program one of the most progressive developmental agendas seen in decades.

The success of this program relies on a strong collaborative network. A key pivot point came when the Government of India recognized that cash is still the main method of transaction and that there was a huge segment of unbanked people living throughout India who had no access to financial services or products. Think of all the least developed and emerging economies where this issue still exists. What the Government of India did was to disrupt the sector by understanding that not everyone could be credit scored; their profile would not suit a traditional bank, and insurance and value-added services were not available, as the costs and type of products probably did not have a fitness of purpose for India. Pramod outlined that where needed he build domestic and international alliances to support the building of one of India's largest urban and rural connected financial networks.

The government launched a twelve-digit unique identification number assigned to every individual resident of India; this single step removed inefficiencies in the ID process. This program will eventually serve as the basis for a database with which disadvantaged Indian residents can access services that have previously been denied to them, due to lack of identification documents.

So, how does one go about reaching and providing services to such a vast number of people? What Oxigen did well was build its services with the customers in mind; it built relationships with local retailers, in villages and towns. It developed products and services beneficial to retailers and customers. A farmer, for example, needs simplicity in terms of technological access, asset protection, and costs that are not prohibitive.

The company has developed several global relationships with leading providers who now engage with the Oxigen platform infrastructure to provide services to a broader customer base who would not normally have access; without this infrastructure, transactions would be complicated, service offering would be limited, at a developmental goal level, social and financial inclusion would not be achieved.

When done correctly, value cascades. Taking Oxigen as an example, here are some stats and facts on India.

- India's Population: 1.3 billion.

- India launches digital authentication program—1.1 billion potential biometric digital IDs.

- 650 million mobile users in India.

- Only 200k ATMs.

- 125k bank branches.

- 30 million merchants in India.

- 94% of the population still transacts in cash

Oxigen current business stats:

- 150 million customers (expected to reach 300 million by 2020).

- 2 billion USD gross transactional value.

- 50 million transactions per month.

- 200k points of access.

- 30 million mobile wallets.

- $1.5 million loaned, business to business base.

- +1.2 million affordable insurance policies issued to the public.

Oxigen has grown to such an impressive scale by collaborating and augmenting its services, ensuring that the services offered are accessible, affordable, and relevant. It has the potential to upscale at unprecedented levels. It makes a difference, and provides access and support economic and social inclusion, acting as a conduit between government, business, and citizens.

For those with developmental goals, how could other countries benefit from the infrastructure which Oxigen has built to support financial, national inclusion mandates? It is fair to say that to scale to the numbers shown above is no easy task, my suggestion is there is tremendous potential for inter-government collaboration. Why waste time trying to reinvent the wheel?

Chapter 3: Commitment

So many people talk about collaboration as if it is a momentary, feel-good philosophy that only works as a concept; from my experience, it is constant and should become ingrained as part of the organizational culture. Similarly, collaboration is not a job that can be assigned to one or two individuals; it is the responsibility of every manager, team leader, and member of the organization that they must display their commitment through a willingness to cooperate with every other person involved. This commitment drives achievement; it is what underpins the pulse of engagement and keeps progress within reach.

When there is no commitment, we experience conformity drift, where people's motives sway or are influenced by the wrong reasons. Group members tend to conform to the majority view, whether they agree with it or not. My advice is simple; it is essential to check that everyone is on board for the right reasons. I am overjoyed when I see different information being shared, and focused actions being self-delegated across teams; what makes no sense is when ideas are prematurely thrown out, and no commitment is given to ensuring that the right kinetics flow.

Collaborative-minded individuals will form teams that draw partners both from inside and outside of their usual group. They have the innate ability to inspire trust among others and engage with those around them in an easy, natural, and friendly manner while treating others with fairness and integrity.

The ability to build, sustain and transform collaborative relationships is an essential skill not based on, or dependent upon, any particular level of education, years of experience, or job title. Instead, they seem to include the following inherent personality traits: being able to relate to others, keeping one's ego at bay, facilitating and encouraging openness, leaving room for novel and alternative options.

When I asked Patrick Gallagher, CEO of City Sprint, the UK's leading final-mile logistics company, "What advice would you give to an aspiring entrepreneur?" Patrick replied, "There are two main pieces of advice I'd share with anyone wanting to start or run their own business. First, you cannot do it yourself, and second, you will only be as good as the sum of all your parts: your team. So, focus, support, and nurture them because it will pay you back again and again if you get it right".

It takes time and a conscious effort to explore the drivers of value, and is a skill helps you unpick the most daunting issues at hand. When we increase self-awareness, we drive further understanding and the dawning of acceptance results in an incredible shift in mindset and clarity of purpose.

We all know that gaining confidence is no easy task, but when we have an excellent conversation it leaves a lasting impression, we resonate and come away with a mutual accomplishment. It's the opposite, however when we engage with people who say one thing then assume they meant something else. Those who rely on ambiguous memos, cutting tweets and snarky comments to make themselves seem important and smart are doing nothing but undercutting their own goals and the progress and livelihoods of others.

Collaboration demands the ability to see not just the here and now, but also the ability to consider the art of the possible and glimpse into the distant future. It requires all to be able to address opportunities as well as deal with precision the inner and outer conflicts we face, and bring into harmony those fiery wills of individual team members. It demands that a leader be aware of the various ways in which their members can disrupt engagement.

I have frequently demonstrated, through my interactions that value exists within and all around us; it is the like the untapped energy of water in a dam, just waiting to be activated. At its simplest level, value flows when we engage through meaning when we let the water through the dam, generating the current of electricity to power mutual exchange. Interactions when done well, drive meaningful dialogue which can break those stubborn and old habits, we possess.

If we are not careful, we can become lost in general dialogue which lacks specificity— this applies to the discussion and interpretation of the context of value, it is one of those aspects which we typically define at an individual level, and as such, it can be subjective in nature; the value one person sees in a new idea or concept can be lost entirely in another individual.

Don't just use the word value for the sake of it, connect and commit to exploring the way value is exchanged between people, teams, and customers. Value is thus both subjective (i.e., a function of someone's estimation) and relational (i.e., where both benefits and cost must be positive values). Most of my time is spent on helping people at all levels to be more mindful especially when we wish to develop and engage with value.

It is difficult to truly make a difference when the operational ecosystem in which you operate is plagued with inefficiencies.

When dealing with or exploring the relativity of value, consider the following:

- Is it explicit or implicit? If it's implicit, it's difficult to pinpoint and sometimes hard to articulate.

- To what degree is value negotiable, do you accept or decline?

- Is there a consensus on the context of value so that everyone is clear, there should be a common understanding?

- Determine how value is exchanged and indexed. Design a value matrix assessment to include: The internal impact, the external impact, the ongoing ripple effect that occurs, its impact on behaviors and motivations, the reduction in risk achieved.

Engagement

The simple fact is that unless we maintain an attitude that fosters equal benefit and value for all parties concerned, effective collaboration becomes nearly impossible. The competitive spirit seems to be hard-wired in many people, such that they will win at all costs. From Sport to Business leaders, we see time and time again blunders which are beyond one's comprehension, playing out.

It's easy to be a naysayer, to criticize, whine, and moan, and find a dozen excuses as to why something, or someone's ideas, won't work. It is particularly easy to be negative when things are not going well, or you are tired or distracted. These things make it easy to become sidetrack and for tensions to rise, but that does not make it right or productive. Reverse the situation, and think about how you feel when someone criticizes your efforts rather than supporting you constructively. It hurts, and you become resentful. Thus, communication breaks down. So, the next time you are tempted to criticize someone, either take a slow, gentle constructive approach or don't say anything at all. Criticism, when called for, should always be constructive and delivered in a measured, friendly, helpful manner.

If, you feel your team is struggling and that momentum is stalled, or it is just lurking under the surface, assess whether it is being bogged down in infighting, turf wars, or a bunker mentality. If you come across this situation, then it is time to take control. Lead the group out of the bunker and into the open. Collaboration and hostility are never a great mix, it is destructive, and like a tornado, uprooting everything, such negative attitudes accomplishes nothing. What does work is the beacons of innovation, the potential promise, rather than hurricanes of confusion, and undue pressure on processes and systems.

What's it like when you know you can make a difference, and others just don't want to listen or when poor interpersonal relationships exist? the value will be hard to precisely state and will be overshadowed by issues which exacerbate the differences. When others don't want to engage, or drive fear, it is intimidating and will reduce the ability for genuine ideas of merit to flow.

Do not assume that the shyness of someone means they cannot interact. Engagement is inclusive; such that it allows diversity of thoughts, personalities, and behaviors to gel and connect. Make sure that ideas do not simply fall in line with those who hold the strongest voice. The best in class collaborator will cajole conversations, empower expressions of value, such that even the quietest voices can be heard.

Exceptional collaborators gently and patiently guide teams forward, the contrast is those who prefer to dictate to get results and trust me this still happens, I hear horror stories at least once a week! In such cases, it results in intellectual laziness and a laissez-faire attitude setting in, without a change and shift, whirlpools of discontent will flow, others who are more agile and relevant will simply pounce and seize opportunities which avail, striking out those who fail to respond and adapt.

For some people, being asked to share leadership responsibilities may induce feelings of fear, awkwardness, and displeasure, and not be naturally comfortable, especially when group members are difficult or unwilling to participate. At the same time, no one enjoys being forced into accepting decisions that they don't understand, nor do they appreciate being sidelined and left out, such dispositions lead to discontent and the complete breakdown of relationships, it becomes impossible to row forward in the same direction.

Thinking in isolation or approaching problems with a bunker mentality inevitably limits progress and stifles creativity. I have found that these situations are brought about by a crisis of trust: a case in which employees, management, and team members have become cynical and suspicious of each other, unsure of who they can trust (or if they can trust anyone at all), and are therefore disinclined to collaborate. In such a toxic atmosphere, people retreat into a defensive mode and cling to the belief that sharing their thoughts and ideas will somehow weaken their power base. This leads to personal turf wars when team members come to the table with an agenda already established, or when one party feels that another individual or the group has invaded their professional, personal, or philosophical territory.

When Politics are at play, all too often, efforts are poorly driven off course and efforts seem to head into the bunkers, unsure of what is happening next. A concerted effort is required to avoid being wiped out, dealing with such diversions requires those who are following you to interpret the situation at hand while maneuvering a path forward.

The successful leader goes out of their way to make sure that political motives have been eliminated from the collaborative process and bring harmony to the situation, thus preventing a rift that might result in a disastrous breakdown of progress.

Engagement will not occur when there is no will to make a difference, think about it, how many times have you been in a position where you wanted to make a difference, but decided that it was too much effort—so you did not even try?

When is the last time you sat in a meeting, said nothing, as power politics was at play, and it resulted in an opportunity slipping past?

Are you ready to Engage?

Power up

The following guidelines enhance synergy development and propel you forward.

1. Understand the benefits of coordination:

In addition to exchanging information and ideas, coordination involves the aligning and arranging of activities in such a way that the desired results are achieved in the most time efficient manner possible.

2. Increase aspects of cooperation:

Ensure that all members are working together efficiently, and are freely exchanging ideas, both as a group and in a quasi-independent manner. Does your style of leadership or management inspire cooperation?

3. Drive collaboration forward:

Collaboration is an extension of cooperation. The collaborative process ensures that all participants share information, resources, and responsibilities jointly and that they work together throughout the planning, evaluation, and implementation stages of a project.

Rushing headlong into discovery and engagement without first establishing realistic, well structured, step-by-step goals, and without taking the time to get to know one another beyond the norms of hospitality will leave gaps in understanding and everyone exposed.

You can enhance creativity and collaboration using these principles and practices:

1. Engagement: Do the people with whom you engage with, have it? Collaboration works best when team members have complementary and diverse skill sets. This will help you access collective intelligence and make informed decisions.

2. Healthy relationships matter: Appreciating others, engaging in purposeful conversations and the ability to resolve conflicts are essential ingredients for collaborations.

3. Guide visions and clarity of purpose count: Clear, common purpose makes everything they do seem meaningful and valuable." Use storytelling to drive synergy and buy in.

4. Agree with your charter/mission: Team members should jointly agree the rules of engagement which include goals, roles, responsibilities, and deliverables.

5. Connect the project with the company's big picture objectives: Create meaning and value for the organization and customers.

6. Nature the brilliance of others: Provide inspiring leadership which nurtures people to excel, build greater connectivity and give credit often.

7. Make a difference and add zest: Be reasonable, listen, open dialogue, be authentic and real.

Chapter 4: Overcoming Overload

I have found that in most cases, 25% of value-added collaborations which occur within businesses come from only 5% of the employee base. If everyone was given the opportunity to unlock their talent, just imagine the influence it would have on productivity and progress? Is there an overload of processes and systems which simply creates a culture of reduced goodwill to flow or is there ineffectiveness of management layers stifling progress which means countering anything that is different?

The best organizations allow people to apply their capabilities performance and reputation. They enable efforts to increase collaborative efficiency across value chains and supply and demand structures. Employee surveys, electronic tools, and internal systems such feedback loops and co-creation programs provide valuable data points which will indicate where the stress points which counterbalance progress.

Collaboration overload occurs when efforts seem to lead to undue pressures on people, such that decisions and progress stalls, and everyone just feels as if they are operating with reoccurring bottlenecks, such experience will also see issues continue to rise. Far more than often it is always a symptom of some deeper organizational pathology. Attempts to liberate unproductive time by employing new tools (for example, Microsoft Teams, Slack, Box will yield little if the underlying issue of poor communication is not addressed. Companies that have successfully combatted such situations have done so by focusing on the root causes and not merely the symptoms—which reduces friction and internal resistance.

There is no gain when we try to build authentic relationships just for the sake of it. All this does is place pressure on those who genuinely want to make a difference, it leads to dissolution and a breakdown in trust. After all, two heads are almost always better than one. But left unchecked, calls for greater collaboration can lead to a culture of "collaboration for collaboration's sake," which is built on false premises.

Addressing root causes

But it doesn't have to be this way. The best companies don't drive workforce productivity by attacking the roots of collaboration. Instead, they take steps to address the underlying causes. They will nature a reduction of tension and support cross-department synergy, in doing so, they will unlock ideas to be shared.

Another type of overload is when other team members don't understand each other, it creates tension, which prevents a lack of meaningful dialogue and indeed no common ground; tension builds into undue stresses, and the weakest points will leak.

Another type of overload is when you feel and experience a constant uphill battle to get your points across to others. In extreme situations, we can become overwhelmed, and relationships, departments, and value systems collapse under the tension of non-cooperation. The pace of progress and acceptance becomes thwarted when partial agreement becomes the norm.

There will be occasions when we have to break free from the shackles of discontent and take control if we wish to make a difference, sometimes this will involve moving out of one ecosystem to one which will value you for who and what you are. Search, connect and reach out – you will be surprised when you do, people and results start flowing your way.

The following list represents a list of challenges presented by drifting team members.

- Lack of clarity of purpose.

- Failure to gain the commitment of team members.

- Failure to accurately identify issues and communicate them.

- Hindered by burdensome, negative experiences.

- Poor facilitation and nurturing of the collaborative spirit.

- Fatigue and relationship drift.

- So, how should we confront some of these problematic situations?

Do not become sidestepped

False confidence, which occurs when you follow everyone else, without giving credence to your independent thinking will often leave you with unsettled in terms of contribution through mutual exchange.

No one likes to operate with a void of purpose, and when objectivity is lost, we operate in a pell-mell mode. The result is confusion, misunderstandings, and ultimately, frustration. The Cure? Engage, contribute, step forward, be objective and focus on the value exchange and the difference you can make.

Many leaders and managers can directly impact success not just for themselves, but their peer groups, colleagues, and coworkers. Could you consider these are additional focus areas for a change?

- Encourage behavioral change.

- Reduce complex reporting lines.

- Streamline processes.

- Develop innovation committees or stealth growth discussions.

- Reward collaboration.

- Unlock the Talent from within.

Chapter 5: Collaborative Leadership Traits

Certain identifiable traits almost always characterize collaborative leadership: super engaged, expressive, intentional and driven by the will to win through involvement. They possess the ability to inspire others toward a common vision, beyond a few well-chosen words, they excite those around them. Think about it, who wants to listen to dull and boring pap talk and be managed by inspiring behaviors and ethics?

The collaborative leader brings inspiration to the table, not just through words but simple yet effective actions; they provide encouragement in times of stress and challenges, offering up helpful suggestions, whilst expressing votes of thanks for a job well done, above all they have a willingness to listen to everyone's ideas and concerns, rather than here their own voices, they quell disagreements as they grow and will not argue points of dispute to death for the sake of it.

These traits become competencies which should guide us; they are the tools we have which will help us unlock those value vaults, the place where intents are held and where promise yields positive outcomes. Another way of highlighting the importance of these traits is to illustrate with an example, how would you feel getting into a car with a driver who is not competent? I am sure you would be hesitant, anxious and apprehensive – you know that the risk is high, you sit there gripping the seat and want to get out as soon as you can. It does not matter if the car is slow or fast, small or large, electric or fuel, the feeling will remain the same. The only way to feel comfortable is to either coach the driver or get out the car!

The established collaborator possesses wisdom and will fade into the background when required; they can drive momentum with stealth even by sitting in the background. They empower others through mutual responsibility. Working styles will vary, adapting to each person and group, to drive transparency amongst members to understand how and why things are happening. As trust grows, bonds are enhanced, decisions become easier and individual choices will become respected.

A collaborative leader understands how to nature and build trust ecosystems, which create rivers of constructive dialogue which are meaningful while accepting the outputs and support of the collective. In some instances, this may prove to be a relatively straightforward endeavor; in others, it may be a bit like herding cats. Thus, it requires a balance of social, emotional and logical intelligence for the collective mind to come together.

I referred to a quote in the introduction by John M Neill, Chairman and group CEO of Unipart, a global firm with revenues of more than $800 million. A further review of the Unipart website demonstrates operating according to The Unipart Way: "Our philosophy of working underpinned by a strong set of guiding principles, supported by tools and techniques that inspire employee engagement, flexibility, and outstanding customer service. The Unipart Way has already been used successfully to unlock the potential of businesses around the world, in almost any sector.

Not only do our customers achieve reduced costs and the elimination of waste, but they also benefit from hundreds of innovative ideas, from genuinely engaged people. Our method of implementing The Unipart Way is not to do it to you; we teach you how to do it yourself, thereby ensuring that we have transferred the knowledge and skills.

I identify competencies as a set of abilities or qualities at a specific level that companies have decided are desirable for their employees to possess. During a potential new employee's interview and assessment process, the degree to which the individual in question owns the specified competencies is used as a series of benchmarks to establish the applicant's suitability to fill a given position.

When we put our competencies together, our chances of success increase. We become stronger when our abilities are combined than relying on those skills in isolation.

Below are listed the primary distinguishing attributes needed

- Balanced motivations.

- The ability to be authentic.

- Not feeling compelled to always be in control.

- The ability to break down social and business barriers.

- The ability to encourage risk-taking, and simultaneously ensure that all such risks are supported by the trust of the group and a sense of security.

- Contextual intelligence, the ability to apply knowledge to real-world scenarios.

- Open sharing of information.

- Managing conflict constructively.

- Developing collaboration strategies built around the human element.

- The ability to envision new possibilities.

- Helping and empowering people to build trusting relationships.

- The ability to operate with a positive aura.

- Being able to handle and solve problems.

- Employing skills and techniques that facilitate collaboration.

- Encourage brainstorming and out-of-the-box thinking to promote new ideas and creative options.

- Develop greater reflective listening, understanding what is being proposed or discussed.

- Use the word "we" rather than "I" to demonstrate the group's mutuality.

- Have the courage to identify and address personal feelings as they arise.

- Make sure multiple ideas and options are proposed and discussed for each phase of the project.

- Take time to clarify the mutual benefits of each potential solution as it is proposed.

- Always provide time for participants to take ideas away with them, reflect on them, and discuss them with outside stakeholders.

- Always commit to enacting a final resolution.

It's worth exploring the concept of ability in a more practical way, so I reached out to Wayne Clarke, founder of Global Growth Institute and International Brand Ambassador for Junior Chambers International, an international association with 170,000 members globally. Wayne has worked with hundreds of organizations globally on breakthrough and transformational programs. His work spans across the private and public sectors, where he helps CEOs and boards build stronger leadership and management capabilities.

Wayne explains: "You may know what you like and what you're good at, but many find it tricky to tell others about skills which would make you world class. Understanding and displaying good management abilities will help to position you for a successful career no matter what level you're starting at. To remain competitive in the world economy, businesses need to develop a new generation of outstanding managers capable of leading people".

Through his work, Wayne has interviewed over 600 CEOs, influential leaders, and HR professionals internationally, identifying twelve essential management competencies that drive growth. These have been distilled into a framework defining the enabling skills that leaders and HR professionals subscribe to.

Wayne contends that there is a direct link between the twelve core modules contained in his world-class management program and the enabling traits that drive collaboration and synergy. I have dovetailed each one to illustrate their relevance and importance.

The twelve world class skills are as follows:

1. 21st century management:

How 21st-century managers think, act and focus their attention to create maximum value in their organization.

2. Optimizing your time:

Use time efficiently and strategically to make the difference between good and excellent management. Do you seize the moment? Is your time utilized strategically?

3. Great goal setting:

The ability to bring others along on the journey. The importance of progress in collaboration is a self and group level concern. Are you creating synergies that are objective?

4. Improved communication:

The skills and techniques used to build momentum and induce buy-in; this could include pitching your ideas, presenting facts, alerting others to key issues.

5. Inspiring appraisals:

Inspiring appraisals are the bedrock of developing and engaging employees, a core competency of excellent management. Giving feedback, honestly and truthfully, are key to enabling trust. Feedback provides the tracks upon which we can place our efforts; it is not one way, it is multi-dimensional, and within the collaboration, it is vital to complete the checks and balances frequently.

6. Better meetings, better results:

How do you contribute? What will great ideas make your meetings more dynamic and productive, turning them into occasions that people enjoy attending? Being involved, participating, engaging, and interacting drives new synergies and bonds.

7. Understanding your customer:

Develop insights that drive better value internally and externally. How can this process drive co-creation? We are all linked; take the time to understand and appreciate your colleagues and the wider audience.

8. Managing up:

Building partnership-based relationships with those who have significant influence across the organization are just as important as relationships within your team. Sharing and engagements spark innovation and build enhanced capacity.

9. Creating a stand-out team:

Creating teams that stand out and make a difference. Strengthen the team in mind and knowledge. A collaborative team will be prominent.

10. Presenting with presence:

How you present your ideas, thoughts, strategizes, messages and tell stories. If we cannot get those vital messages across, our efforts will take a detour as different interpretations strike home.

11. Developing me, developing my team:

The development toolkit: what's in it for you and your team? Your unique role and contribution, blending and working with others to achieve a win-win.

12. Being a strategic leader:

Thinking strategically and making an impact on organizational growth. The collaborative leader designs efforts and will drive interactions internally and externally. Purposeful intentions will always provide direction.

These twelve world-class managerial skills directly feed into the dialogue of making a difference. They are tried, tested, and respected. They are not simply one-time fixes but will remain with you throughout your career. They can be mastered, and are proven to enhance personal and business growth. These are highly transferable, lifelong skills. What's more, they cut across all levels of seniority and should never be underestimated.

I would highly recommend going through Wayne's online program, which is valuable and relevant to all of us at every level and sector. More information can be found at www.worldclassmanager.com. To join the World Class Managers online global program, why not collaborate now and send a note to the founder, Wayne Clarke at wayne@the-ggi.com.

What strikes you the most from this Chapter?

Chapter 6: Seize The Moment

How many times in each of our lives have we seen brilliant ideas which we generate come to nothing? How often have these been your own ideas? Have you allowed moments of inspiration to wither away? Why is it that at times when important decisions should be made, we sit on the fence through inaction?

Perhaps as you were sharing them, no one else seemed to grasp the concept or did not give it the due attention it deserves. Or was it because you were you unable to explain yourself clearly and concisely? Was your audience not paying attention? Could it be that they failed to see the opportunities that were inherent in your idea as clear as you could? Any of these explanations may be true, but the fundamental, underlying question is: Why does this happen, and what can we do to change it, more importantly, will you change it?

It's one thing others not acting on it, and another if you did not act on an idea you had. What held you back, such that you were unable to step forward? Brilliant ideas and moments of opportunity are fleeting things; once they have passed, the clear majority of them cannot be recaptured. Consider how many sparks of inspiration you have had, promising yourself that you would write it all down, and completely losing the essence of it, when you do. It dawns on you, and reality intervenes; you became distracted, and the great idea, along with the chance to make it happen, slipped away never to be recovered.

We need to tune into opportunities and insights you will establish that they manifest as powerful "AH Ha" moments. It is vital to develop mechanisms that not only help us remember, articulate and engage; so, that they help those creative elements of wonder express and inspire further new actions. Think about it: How do you feel when you are inspired through the actions, attention and recognition provided by another person? What's the feeling like? in such circumstances we want to make a difference, you reciprocate and a new wave of energy sets in, and those barriers which hold us back are reduced.

All too often, our emotional limitations and the fear of trying holds us hostage; we need to break such cycles to move beyond these timorous natures. Once we free ourselves from our insecurities, it renders us mobile and active to reach out to others, we will not feel hemmed in and will start to form new bonds and uncover new opportunities.

The first step to catching and seizing the moment is to understand the construct of realization; to remain firmly anchored in the present while envisioning the possibilities offered by the future. The most significant changes in our lives must begin with small shifts in our state of mind. Even the most mundane activities can provide unexpected opportunities if we teach ourselves to recognize every possibility to affect change and the relative value of those insights, or AH-Ha moments we have.

- Are you able to recognize an Insight when it rises from your mind?

- Can you seize the moment and follow its trail to unlock its value?

- Do you have the key/code or is it held by someone else?

- If all you do is ponder and over analyze – how will you ever feel the moment?

Chapter 7: Gems Of Value

It is essential to discover the brilliance of our minds, but far too often innovation, solutions to problems are hidden within not just ourselves but that of our team members and peer groups. Without a sense of where to head, we search for them as if we are looking for a gem in the pit of rocks, some could be small and others are boulders. The search continues, efforts of turmoil, we work one inch at a time, sometimes on our own and others with a team, tremendous efforts are required to turn over tons of debris, to find one stone of value. This is the same case as our minds, and figments of imagination, we have to turn over thousands of thoughts in the day to turn one over which is a gem. The greatest of gems are quarried out, gold veins are followed until their source reveals the reservoir of value and potential. A diamond is never sitting there in broad daylight; it takes time and patience to take it from its rough form to gleam in all its glory, a skilled craftsman whose love and vision takes it and turns it to a sparkling delight.

Great collaborators who consistently generate many high-performance teams have become skilled in knowing where to find and unlock the minds and passions of those in the team, in doing so taking ideas and intents which glimmer with potential into trinkets of value, even if it is not evident to the eye of others. Remember that a newly-mined diamond looks like any other rock; only when it is cut, and polished does its real value become evident. Provide the care, attention, and skill to allow talent and passion to shine.

Many tons of earth and sweat toiled does not mean that we will strike it rich. Likewise, we should filter out and sift those ideas which stand out and stun us, we will queue up and look at them as they dazzle our minds, from the showcase. Nearly every pathway to some new and desired place is strewn with rocks, and as we walk forward, there will be times we may step on something that causes discomfort—in such case, you are alerted and pay attention to where we walk and start to pay attention. We will come across many discomforts as we move forward, we will need to adjust to problems and challenges, and overcome these obstacles. Many individuals simply accept the presence of these barriers because they have always been there.

Learning how to deal with these rocks, and understanding how to spot the ones that can be turned into a diamond of an opportunity, is a developed skill that takes patience and care.

When you learn the skill of seeing and finding those gems of an idea, it leaves an ecstatic and rewarding feeling. Often, thoughts are on display, some will stand out, while others will appear dull and clunky, uninviting to say the least. Another way to look at this is to consider the lighting that is used in a jewelry store, which when shone on the diverse collection of gems dazzle and come alive. Perhaps it is one stone or many which strike us with the vibrancy of color, which show us those stunning features of creativity. We will have many different gems within our teams, different backgrounds, which will catch our eye, are your eyes open?

Indeed, there may be times when we need to look at people and the tasks they must achieve differently. When we do, new aspects can catch our attention, and we can develop new insights that were previously unseen. A dull cabinet will never make a gem shine. If you are surrounding a gem with a negative or indeed dull expression, it will never shine, imagine going to the jewelry to buy a ring in a bad mood, it will be difficult to ever come out with anything of value. Be the light and illuminate everyone around you. No amount of light will make dull thoughts radiate, yet, this is what we find when we explore some of those great ideas, many of which are simply laying hidden and unnoticed, it is only when they are given some due care and attention, does their true value and glimmer shine through.

I recall designing a national capacity building project for the National Bus Service for the Government of Mauritius – I trained 20 or so Technical and Vocational Trainers. The goal was to drive a culture shift, and create new ways of thinking and collaboration between Bus Drivers and Conductors, and with different departments of the value chain. I spent one month traveling the entire route, length and breadth of this beautiful island as a passenger day and night, covering all quarters. I got to experience the moods, challenges and different issues across the day, I assessed how different passenger groups interacted as they stood at the bus stops, as well as expecting mothers, and the elderly. I looked at the dynamics between the driver and the conductor, and I can say it was a remarkable experience – I had so many questions – which itself had many variables – the biggest one I had related to my goal was, how to do I connect the learning experience required to shift minds and culture to over 2600 individuals, who I do not know, through these specially selected vocational trainers I was asked to mentor and coach.

I reached into my inner competency toolkit, and out jumped my creative streak - I had an idea, in fact, I had many, it was one of those strong impulses, where my intuition kicked in, I just knew that the idea should be followed, seized upon, no matter how rough, do not give up it, is what I remember reflecting. I kept saying to myself; it can't be easy doing their job, the heat, the rain, the sheer numbers at certain times of the day. I had one idea of how to relate and maneuver the key messages required to effect change.

There was one thought which seemed to stick constantly; it stood out, it was vivid, that gem of an idea, that no matter which way I looked it, it seemed to appeal to me, I am sure we have had those ideas which are burning questions. I wondered what the crew did up and down the country during their tea breaks and lunch period. For those who have been to Mauritius, you will note, that buses are quite typical in their look and feel, some small and others are large coach style formats. The crew were always calm, but, I am sure they had a voice!

I followed this query and train of thought, and I did not give up, what I found was that at each lunchtime the crew would sit with other crew members, often in the shade and talk, read newspapers, etc. It was informal dialogue, but they were expressive – whereas they were duty bound and operated by hand signals for most of the day. They were alert, they possessed social intelligence, sharing jokes, even lunches – they supported each other. I could not view them as them and us – they talked, they laughed, they operated as a two-man team, so what was important was to build on the value of trust – it stuck in my mind, they collaborated every day.

The challenge was that the higher authorities who commissioned me to drive the culture change wanted to make sure that the trainers could relate, I had to come up with a way in which I could connect, to share, to move from formal to informal training – My idea, was novel – it had never been done before – I would use collaborative learning as the glue to connect everyone. But, before I could take the trainers on the journey, I had to equip them with the skills to collaborate in the learning journey, to remove those dominant expressions of tell and authority to one of expression through experiential sharing– I sent the trainers on a day out to also experience the challenges and working environment, the instructional design was critical. What I came up with was truly inspirational – I knew that bonds are broken and made when people communicate. We know that fun and appreciation sit side by side, my revelation, was to create a game, it was a gem of an idea, that diamond in the rough. As I polished the idea, it came alive, proximity and casual learning, where the drivers and conductors could relate, where the trainers would form part of the game, by using pictures and expressions on the cards, route numbers, drivers and conductor's places of interest, I created a game of whit, where teams would challenge each other to solve their own problems.

I was given the most experienced trainers, who would provide a consistent experience across all learning groups. I placed the outcomes of the game into a bespoke designed skills passport – and each person filled out key areas they learned and appreciated. Many had never traveled abroad, so having a document which looked like a passport was novel and aspirational. They were proud to see their own name on their passports, it created an emotional bond, something they owned.

It was a huge hit, for many reasons –the program resulted in 100% monitoring and evaluation – I ended up with a log of 2600 attendees – which provided management with different perspectives and ideas to support future innovation – The senior leadership team were taken back by the quality of feedback and more importantly it was in each participant writing. Each page was called a skills visa, a record of what participants learnt, in their own handwriting was recorded, as such, there could be no dispute as to the learning outcomes.

By breaking the course down into a game, we added fun into the mix, the leadership team said it was brilliant. The trainers would follow the same game, and used it to deliver key messages consistently– each trainer was asked to meet and greet attendees outside the workshop rooms, each session the trainers stood outside – greeted, had tea and cakes, a deliberate action to break down barriers and mingle to break down barriers to learning, it was a huge hit with the trainers and attendees. Waves of discussions flowed, the tide of ideas and feedback was overwhelming – as each group went back to their depots, the word spread, it was brilliant – the unions got behind it – they embraced the program, and it was so smooth sailing from there on.

What was amazing was the comments received from the attendees – some people had worked their entire lives in the job, it had young and old – they had a voice, and for many they could express themselves freely in a conducive environment – the gratitude was motivating – the sense of achievement, the sharing – there were many who shone, who surprised everyone – guiding, sharing, collaborating with the trainers to ensure that everyone's voice was heard.

The game idea was not just about having fun; it was about ensuring that we activated the social construct I had seen when they were at lunch. I needed the trainers not to speak down, their goal was to adopt the style I had shown them, to allow them to engage, otherwise the barriers would go up – what is also worthy of mention is that when I took the brief, I was informed there was a high risk that the attendees would not understand English, so the program needed to be delivered in local dialect, in Mauritius people speak Creole at home and French in the workplace.

Here is what happened on Day 1 – The program was developed to such a high standard, the instructional design uplifted dialogue, it allowed ideas and views to be expressed – against the backdrop of appreciation of their roles and tasks, and the pressures they faced, I could relate to them as they spoke about them, remember, I had experienced many of them during my month-long travel on the island, and when the crew realized I was that lone passenger, they laughed and said, "we remember you".

At the first training session, I led the program, allowing the trainers to be part of the attendee group – within minutes everyone was laughing, sharing – working together, and then the penny dropped –what happened stunned us all, drivers and conductors took the lead and embraced our style, every single attendee not only spoke in English but some of them – were so good at presenting that they were as good as some of the trainers, expressive, passionate and would support our theme of change, the trainers did not need to use flip charts – attendees would take the lead and chart their learning, ideas, and feedback on them. Every single group and training session over the course of a few weeks resulted in streams of flip charts being sent to us, pages and pages of innovations, improvements, considerations – recommendations, sub-working committees were formed. I remember the trainers phoning me, saying, you cannot believe the impact, it is one of the most rewarding programs they have ever had to deliver and the Human Resource Development Council the National body praised me for the ability to unlock a new tide of change.

Worthy of mention is that some attendees had never attended an external workshop training program before, but their voices become heard. The essence of the story is that we should never underestimate the talent and skills of those present, and when we understand how to activate minds and connect, something remarkable happens – the brilliance of others and gems start to shine. Collaboration fuels learning and change.

I helped Unlock the Talent from Within –my ethos and theme is always "Collaborate to Win".

Ready to collaborate to win - are you a gem of value?

Chapter 8: Choose The Right People

Don't assume that everyone on the team will automatically understand their role, or instantly fit into some preconceived niche to which they have been assigned. Also, don't fall into the trap of thinking that everyone is going to be able to be the right fit, it takes time to nature cohesion and to have the right people doing the things they are passionate about within existing organizational structures.

If team members do not feel comfortable and confident enough to open and speak candidly in group discussions, brainstorming sessions, and workshops, progress will become impossible. Inevitably, people will have aspects they are motivated to work on, and when you have a wide extended group who have diverse interests and skills, those range of interests and motivational levels will vary, yet, you will be required to build real relationships of value. There are two camps, the coherent and incoherent who prefer to sit on the sidelines. Sometimes the addition of one team member is all that is required to rebalance a team and bring about alignment and synergy. So, what is it you look for when you want to drive value? To me, engagement is stronger when people feel they can contribute and are an integral part of the overall process. Choose people with the right attitude vs. the best qualification!

When we place the right people in the collaborative ecosystem, we can create endless possibilities. In doing so, we strengthen the collective mind which ultimately drives synergies. The collected mind is where we brainstorm and solve solutions; it is where the unspoken word is present and binds together individual intents.

What sort of person is required in your team to make a difference and what are the qualities needed to perform?

Worthy of mention

The best collaboration takes place when a self-organizing team holds universal core values that are embraced and demonstrated in the group's daily encounters. These core values must include mutual trust, respect, participation, and commitment. Those who tend toward adaptive thinking are adept at taking existing context and ideas, refine them, and move easily in new directions.

Assemble a list of possible participants who have something of value to add to the team membership. Try to select those with a range of views, experiences, motivations, and skill sets that are appropriate to the project at hand. Not everyone chosen for the team will be able to contribute, but there are a few guidelines you can follow that will help you achieve a healthy balance.

Choose people who are dedicated to the cause and have an intrinsic motivation to engage in the collaborative process. Next to dedication, sector-specific knowledge and experience are the greatest assets members can bring to the team. Some team members will be more adept as visionaries who can see the big picture, and move from one point of view to another as the need arises. Others are more pragmatic in their approach to problem-solving, breaking problems down into their component parts, proposing practical plans of action, and making problems easier to deal with.

Do not fail to continue the relationship-building process, get teams aligned to work on specific projects and if necessary, change them around until they find the correct balance of output and dialogue. When the right arrangement is reached and plans come together, any resistance is reduced. Reaching this point requires effort if you expect optimal results. While this process may appear to some as an unnecessary waste of time, it brings tremendous benefits throughout the collaborative process.

Once you have chosen your team members, it is critical to get the team running and working together toward a common goal as quickly and efficiently as possible. The ability to accomplish this seemingly ordinary and mundane task can be far more complicated than most people realize, and it is not a job for the faint of heart. It is one thing to identify these individuals, and quite another to gain their commitment and convince them to engage freely and openly with other team members so that they can make a difference.

Sometimes it's ok to add people or it may be reasonable to break a team into smaller focused working groups, rearranging members so that they can contribute and drive value additions. There is no point in having the teams all made up of the same sort of mindset, this far often than not leads to progress stalling. The point is that we need diversity and people with common interests to coexist and provide a mix of abilities. Achieving the right mix may require several shuffles.

While keeping, their team focused on the straight and narrow path toward their goal; the effective collaborator must also be a visionary, guiding teams toward an improved future filled with boundless possibilities. Remaining upbeat even when things are not going well, keeping the group focused on the big picture (on their goal and in the future), and congratulating and celebrating even small successes all serve to strengthen team commitment and guard against discouragement and burnout.

In many ways, the leader must act as a cheerleader. When facilitating engagement, there must be a continual nudge towards the idea that it is best to aim for a win-win situation even when issues are faced or group boredom sets in. Perhaps frayed tempers, burnout and outside opposition will drive a win-lose, or lose-lose position if the team loses sight of this. A word of caution: egos and frustration must never be allowed to overpower enthusiasm and dedication to the purpose of the collective.

The whole concept of a collaborative team becomes useless if the team members are always at loggerheads and therefore unable to contribute effectively to achieving the group's stated goal. Vigorous debate is encouraged, but petty infighting is a destructive force that can quickly ruin the work of weeks, and possibly destroy everything the team has managed to accomplish.

The collaborative environment can be cultivated and facilitated by following the following steps:

1. Communicate expectations:

Collaboration does not need to be ad-hoc. The team leader should help team members define their roles and responsibilities within the team, in such a way that they will, henceforth, take responsibility for the outcome of their own work.

2. Set team goals:

Establish concise, measurable goals for the team and review the progress toward these goals at fixed intervals, not to exceed quarterly. Publish the results of the reviews so that everyone knows how the project is progressing and has physical evidence of the progress.

3. Foster a creative atmosphere:

Provide the group with a non-judgmental framework in which issues and obstacles are viewed merely as challenges that need to be met and overcome. Nurture a can-do attitude. Encourage character development and cohesion of minds and efforts.

4. Learn about others:

Different personality dynamics, skill sets, backgrounds, and experiences are and should be present in every team effort. It is worth the effort to have each member complete a simple personality profile that can be shared with the team so that everyone is aware of the other members' strengths.

As a quick check, do these following traits reflect your current approach?

- We are good at practicing inclusiveness.

- Our culture is open to trying out new ideas from unusual or unlikely sources.

- We do not have an issue changing course when the situation demands it.

- It's ok to let go of ideas and courses of action that are not working.

- We enjoy creating new opportunities for greater participation.

- Our approach reflects the desire to protect the integrity of our efforts and decisions.

If the answer is no to any of the above, then it's time refocus and strategize. Each of these is essential keys for collaborative effectiveness.

Do you have the right people in your team?

Chapter 9: The Power Of Influence

I want to concentrate for a moment on the power of influence. The influence you have on other people and those who can influence you in any given situation, the problem at hand, or even on how they look at life itself. Influence, like power, is a neutral force when balanced; it can be used for either good or evil, depending upon how the person exerting it wields it and how we ourselves perceive it. Little can be achieved without the ability to influence others.

- Do some people respond or react?

- Why do some people tend to support you and others just ignore?

- What is it about you that wins people over to your ideas?

- How do we cooperate and when does collaboration truly work?

- What binds the synergy and connections that you, what is the common value thread that exists.

- Is there something about your manner and presence which sways people?

To gain the success you seek influence will without a shadow of a doubt play a big part of it. This involves developing your personal power. We all want people to think positively about what we do, for people to listen to you, to hear you out and accept either your point of view of observations, when we don't achieve this, it's demoralizing as we feel that our ideas are not accepted and do things that you need them to do. We may need to influence someone else about a decision they are taking or it could be that you wish to influence decisions for example, when presenting yourself at an interview or at a meeting.

Do not assume that there will be no further bumps in the road. We can fall into a state of disarray without realizing it has happened. Even the most dedicated team can quickly lose its way, becoming derailed amid the sea of minutiae with which it is forced to deal, and end up trapped in endless rounds of meetings, which become ever more meaningless and frustrating. Integral to this process is the leader's ability to assign clear, concise decisions, rights, and responsibilities, including the mandate to end discussions when the appropriate time comes. In this way, the tendency toward endless, circular argument or discourse can be circumvented and tempers which are frayed to the point that they degenerate into shouting matches can be reduced and managed. When it becomes evident that no consensus has been, or is likely to be, reached, note matters of import and direct discussions towards the objective.

For me, one of the strongest assets required is the ability to connect and influence where you have to join the dots together, when done well, you will win minds and hearts – as you shape decisions. It is a power station when positive energy flows and lights up everyone, everything in your grid is enlightened, self-esteem rises, and the recognition bestows you. When it's negative energy – it is dark and destructive and pulls everything and everyone down.

Influence comes from within and from our external interaction, it has many variables, those which hinder and those that propel. We can shift our progress and prosperity through influencing the things which matter the most. People with power don't need to be overly political. There is as mentioned the negative and positive influence - Take, for example, the contrary position some people take or that false news which is spread and indeed political propaganda. When we hear the word propaganda, we almost instinctively think of a destructive, negative influence distorting the truth, making a situation appear far more dangerous and ugly than it is. This can be true. But it is equally true that there is positive propaganda, which can have a positive influence on those who hear its message.

Don't ever give up if others try to malign you; not everyone will have the same intentions or values that you have. Whether it is the influence of so-called propaganda, or the subtle influence of an individual's words, actions, or deeds, the input we all receive and absorb daily can change how we see the world and how we react to day to day situations. To exert any influence on others, we must establish criteria that encourage change, hopefully of a positive nature. To make this influence work, we must first establish a personal connection, a bond of trust, that makes the recipient willing to accept the influence of someone else. It is this ability to create links that make some individuals vastly more effective at instilling their own values into those around them than other people can.

In the world of business and politics, those who can exert the greatest amount of influence on others are viewed as a highly valuable commodity. Such people typically fall into certain specific categories; some are positive contributors, innovators, and motivators. However, it is my advice to leaders to look beyond these particular groups and reach out to anyone who is willing to engage, share, and participate. In doing so, we can link together chains of people, ideas, methods of doing things, and resources in ways that will encourage positive actions.

Of course, there will always be those who have this talent innately or can develop it, and there are those for whom it will always remain an elusive dream. We will come across those who are active and vocal, and those who will, for whatever reason, remain silent.

As you find your own level in this maze of doing, participating, and stepping back, it is of paramount importance that you can be relied upon to keep your word. Avoid taking on too many responsibilities, because there is a limit to both human endurance and the number of hours we can work. If you allow yourself to become overcommitted, things will begin to fall apart you will fail at everything and be subject to burnout. By contrast, when you commit yourself to doing something, always follow through.

Curiously, many companies spend inordinate amounts of time, energy, and money attracting talented new employees, only to force them into roles and a corporate culture or department which kills all creativity and cripples their ability to engage. Likewise, left to their own devices, people will tend to cling to those individuals and ingrained ways of doing business that inhabit their own comfort zone. Thus, they are missing out on vast opportunities, deadly for those wishing to innovate.

One of the key ways of growing greater influence is to focus on building your personal power of awareness and remember Power doesn't equal politics, so you don't become a Machiavellian character nor betray integrity!

In a nutshell

- Influence is about being aware of the outcome and begin with the end in mind.

- Power is internal and specific to you; it is driven from within, the mindset, the values, and context – it is a chosen path which motivates actions and thinking.

- Politics are the chosen behaviours which people use to influence the thoughts and direction of others (either positive or negative). Do not play with people's aspirations and livelihoods.

Don't underestimate your ability to influence, your own personal influence and power, become less dependent on the use of political motives to generate influence and success. If the leader appears to be playing politics or is defensive, the rest of the team will inevitably do the same. You can't efficiently collaborate if you bring such mindset and ethos to the table – I prefer diplomacy - It is vital to avoid those corrosive effects of tribalism and politics, which can sometimes creep into collective dialogue. When it does, the leader must be able to identify it immediately and move to stifle it before it infects progress.

Where does your greatest influence stem from?

Chapter 10: The Collaborative Ego

One of the greatest challenges you may face is having to overcome reticence, infighting, petty politics. There are always those who will scoff, denigrate, mock, and demean both whatever goal the team is aiming toward and the efforts of the team leader. Do not let this deter you. Some people just delight in tearing down anything that others are trying to build. Such people are not worthy of your attention, so don't let them distract you from your goals.

A common sign that the collaborative process is careening out of balance is when participants begin jockeying to enhance their own positions, making power plays and engaging in the all-too-common corporate mentality of the big fish eating the little fish. Such political games will not only slow the overall progress of the group, but they can also permanently damage the group's functionality by offending less aggressive members of the group and making them feel personally diminished. I refer to this disastrously one-sided phenomenon as collaborative ego.

If the corrosive effects of collaborative ego take root, the positive effects of synergy are lost. Progress toward the ultimate goal will falter, and it will become difficult, if not impossible, to recover the proper balance. Reining in and balancing the level and degree of input and control of each participating member of a collaborative group—and keeping dialogue relevant, on track, and mutually beneficial—will help prevent collaborative ego taking hold.

Solving problems as soon as they appear, rather than ignoring them until they reach the crisis point, will help prevent an imbalance in the dialogue and ensure that things keep progressing smoothly.

True synergy is not driven, nor achieved, by instituting a set of artificially imposed mile markers on the group's efforts. When a rigid step-by-step system is enacted, enthusiasm will wane, and all progress will fizzle out. Synergy is a living thing; it can only be achieved by a dynamic input from partners who are genuinely involved in a continuing process of tearing down barriers and sharing information, creating a free exchange of ideas.

So, how can we work towards achieving these goals and increase synergy in the process?

Form value creation teams

Businesses and other groups should establish cross-business think tanks and innovative value management creation teams, tasked with developing and implementing a flexible, but repeatable, management process that is committed to discovering and maintaining a value-based system. Such groups should be formed carefully, with all members being integrated into the whole with the greatest care.

Establish foundational processes

These processes will guide the value creation teams so they can devote their creative energy to work, rather than to procedures. This overall framework must include a plan of engagement both internally and externally and should include cross-enterprise governance models to encourage interaction, organizational redesign to institute necessary changes, and protocols for measuring and sharing value, innovation assessment, and prioritization.

Manage the transformation

This ensures that the time, effort and money invested in various endeavors undertaken by the team will pay the proper dividends. It includes establishing procedures that ensure knowledge and information are appropriately transferred from place to place in a timely and efficient manner, and performance is measurable, all communications are properly managed and archived.

What're your thoughts on ego?

Chapter 11: Cooperate vs. Collaborate

The concept of collaboration is frequently confused with that of cooperation; while they are often assumed to be synonymous, they are two different things.

Just as too little collaboration and cooperation lead to a complete inability to get anything accomplished, too much collaboration without a correct foundation and system can result in endless rounds of meetings, discussions, and debates in the struggle to reach some elusive consensus.

I recently reached out to Daniel Burrus, who is considered one of the world's leading futurists on global importance and whom The New York Times has referred to as one of the top three business gurus in the highest demand as a speaker. Burrus has frequently cited the differences between collaboration and cooperation, and noted the importance of having meaningful discussions and conversation (communication) to support strong team engagement.

In Burrus' February 22, 2017, article, "3 Steps to Build a Strong Team", on his blog the second step is to Collaborate, Don't Just Cooperate, he wrote:

"The terms collaborate and cooperate, might seem somewhat similar, but their differences are both distinct and meaningful. It's amazing how many companies and organizations say they are collaborating when they are only cooperating. That's because they don't know the difference, and in this case, the difference can make all the difference".

"People cooperate because they have to and because they have to, the focus is on protecting and defending their piece of the economic pie. It's a strategy based on scarcity".

"On the other hand, people collaborate because they want to. You choose to collaborate because you understand that by working together you can create a bigger pie for all. It's inclusive and expansive".

Collaboration, on the other hand, is a purposeful relationship in which two or more parties strategically choose to cooperate to achieve shared or overlapping objectives. Sometimes called a 'win/win' strategy, the collaborating style strives to make sure that both sides are satisfied. It requires an open discussion of all the issues and concerns, exploration of alternative solutions, and honesty and commitment from all the parties. To be successful, the collaborating style participants need to be able to surface concerns in a non-threatening way and think imaginatively.

By creating a commitment to shared goals, we reduce negativity. Where there is clarity of purpose, efforts will shift towards overcoming whatever conflicts arise. Those who understand how to empower such interaction drive speed, efficiency, adaptability, productivity, and innovation. The most productive leaders embody positivity, exude unwavering enthusiasm, and have this knack for finding a way forward when others cannot.

Be sure you understand the difference between a compromising style and a collaborating style: compromising is 'horse-trading,' giving up things you want in the hopes that the other side will do the same and that you can live with the outcome. In collaboration, both sides are trying to find a solution which truly satisfies the needs of each.

Active collaboration takes place when mechanisms, structures, processes, and skills are available to bridge both organizational and personal differences in such a way that it will lead to enhanced communication, coordination, control, and relationships. Unlike cooperation, this collaboration should produce a win/win situation for all parties concerned, as everyone is driven to make a difference.

The collaborative atmosphere is not simply strategic but is also motivated by an understanding of, and respect for, the other participants' respective goals. A willingness to listen with an open mind to alternative ideas and views, and to trust one's fellow team members, is essential if any collaboration is to be successful.

Thus, while cooperation may prevent conflict, it is not nearly as mutually beneficial as is collaboration. It takes each one of us working toward a common goal to make a difference that will benefit us all. It is in this collaborative process that life's unsung heroes lie; people who have been powerful agents for change, who have helped build new communities and shape the future in new and positive ways.

Worth mentioning here are our own unique and individual cooperation/conflict tendencies, which are the basis of the highly acclaimed global personality assessment known as the Thomas-Kilmann Conflict Mode Instrument (TKI). For more than forty years, the Thomas-Kilmann assessment test has been used by human resources (HR) and organizational development (OD) consultants to determine how conflict-handling modes affect personal, group, and organizational dynamics.

Ralph Killmann, a co-founder of this assessment, cites numerous studies and extensive research that demonstrate how a range of traits interact when we are faced with a conflict: a situation we know will arise when we work with teams or larger cooperatives.

The TKI identifies five behavioral dimensions that fall within an assertiveness and cooperativeness matrix. Three of the aspects are cooperative in nature: collaborating, compromising, and accommodating. Those traits that are conflict dimensioned are designated as competing and avoiding. To highlight how these opposites, relate to each other, take each of these traits and think about the times you shift between collaboration and conflict.

Think about it, do you sometimes compromise your efforts by surrendering your position to please someone else? Do you accommodate others, trying to keep everyone happy? Or when challenged, do you compete to win at all costs, or avoid any form of conflict and just go with the flow?

I strongly recommend you review these traits and do a quick self-assessment, remembering that our self-perception can often wrong.

The Thomas Killmann assessment and its associated tools have helped millions of people around the world. In fact, more than 8,000,000 copies have been published since 1974. I reached out to Ralph recently, and he shared some excellent insights. He directed me to his armory of blogs and tools, which are available for anyone who is interested in learning about how they operate in both natural and conflict based situations.

I asked a leading HR Practitioner based in the Gulf, Damian John, to share his views on collaboration. His own career reflects the notion, "when there is a will, there is a way" and one he cites as being pivotal to his own rise through the ranks and one which has been at the forefront of his efforts. He is currently responsible for Group Level Human Capital Development at the Al Harshar Group of Companies, a significant brand and business conglomerate based in the Sultanate of Oman.

Damian is someone I trained many years ago, in fact, thinking about it, there are quite a few people globally whose careers have been positively influenced after attending one of my training programs, they come from all walks of life, and with a far spectrum of skills, some with limited experience have become master practitioners.

Interestingly, as I am writing this, a thought emerged, when I think of it, quite a few people I have trained have become international experts, and there are also Chairman's and CEO's I have worked for, who years later have become my clients. In both cases synergy, cooperation, and a collaborative mindset maintained momentum, and while the tables were turned, value has been exchanged.

I posed the question to Damian, in today's context, how does collaboration sit as an agenda item within the HR Landscape, and human capital agenda? Damian emphasizes that growth is hard to achieve when people or departments are operating as those ever-present "grips of silo." He said everyone talks about teamwork and collaboration, finding ways to relate to the age-old syndrome, of linking their efforts to the leader's declared vision, mission, and expected behaviors. To support this linkage, he says, "We can't grow unless we collaborate, it is a central theme at all levels within our business. We use collaboration to drive personal innovation, and it is a key tactic used to shift efforts from Employee Engagement to an Employee Experience.

The "Employee Experience," is an ecosystem that integrates three core dimensions: engagement, culture and performance management – it is where collaboration sits center stage, and where the experience drives behavioral change.

Nathan Kelleher, Vice President of Global Carrier Strategy Neopost Shipping, provided an excellent summary when I asked him his views on collaboration. To paraphrase: when you build Collaborative networks or communities, they should be designed such that those within can apply their unique talents to areas of interest and related projects—it drives a motivated collective mission. It allows for an inspired common purpose to grow organically, mobilizing the talents and emotional intelligence of those involved. This results in highly manageable working groups. Far too often, organizations try to strike a tricky balance between short-term top-line numbers, and long-term relationships.

What strikes you most from this Chapter?

Chapter 12: Being World Class

To me, our frames of reference are only as good as what we wish to see or perceive them as–and is only as relevant as the way we chose to think and feel. Certificates or accolades alone do not bind it, neither does the amount of funds you hold in your account – it reflects a deeper value, the sincerity, and loyalty, is the true currency of value you hold. It is how your actions no matter how trivial or small, influences and impacts others. I have come across hundreds of people who are not in the press or who have built billion dollar enterprises, many an unsung hero everyday making a difference acknowledged only through their local efforts, filling the hearts and spirits of those in need with acts of devotion and sincerity.

Being world class, reflects one's actions the impact they have, irrespective of class, color and creed – it is present when there is a genuine concern for yourself and others. It is when we get to that point of giving something back, no matter how small or a gesture, everything counts. As eluded, it is beyond accolade or accomplishments and achievements. Think about all those small compliments which are given and those random acts of kindness which brighten up someone who is less fortunate or in a difficult situation. These heroes are passionate about what they do, sincere and humble, their acts of kindness hit home, their goodwill is countless.

Do you demonstrate a genuine sense of enthusiasm, is our presence genuinely felt such that it encourages care or concern for those around us, are we sympathetic to those in need of support – when we are the return is tenfold. Above all, be genuine in your dealings with others. The knack of being yourself, of coming across as open and honest, is an essential part of being true to your own ideas and engaging in successful collaboration with others.

Putting on a different face for each group of people—friends, family, co-workers, subordinates, superiors, and acquaintances—is both exhausting and frivolous. One's demeanor and respect for others should always remain consistent. Otherwise, the facades will start to crack, and people will start to think of you as a person who must have something to hide: one who is so uncomfortable with themselves will place a different mask on to be accepted. Simply put, don't be a phony; always be yourself.

The simple act of avoiding partisanship can inspire true confidence. In the same way that it is important to be good to others, it is essential that we all learn to admit our flaws and accept that we will have flaws and we are prone to make mistakes, learn from them and be better. None of us is perfect, so accept your shortcomings and admit to those mistakes we make, no matter how trivial. Humility and honesty will encourage a deeper level connection which transcends you and those around you.

An essential part of having active one-on-one connections with others is the ability to be a good listener. Anyone can listen to another person speak, but are you hearing what they are saying? Effective collaboration depends on the ability to comprehend another's words and understand the meaning behind them. When someone talks to you, make eye contact, particularly if they are opening about their personal feelings or concerns. Ask follow-up questions to show that you were paying attention to their words and that you care about them as a person.

Above all, learn to share. This is something that we routinely teach children, but it is just as important for us as adults. But unlike children sharing their toys, we need to learn to share our inspirations and influences. Be willing to tell people about those individuals, experiences, and things that helped shape you into the person you are today so that they, too, might benefit.

When you share your experiences, particularly when they involve others who have been part of your journey, we in doing so, resonate a new form of influence which cascades our inner sanctuary and presence of mind and purpose. No matter who you are or how much you have accomplished, recognize those who have supported you along the journey. This will resonate with everyone who sees and feels your passion for making a difference.

Being World Class allows you a seat at the table no matter where and who are you. Make a difference and be that difference, do your best and be sincere to your cause and that of others.

73

Chapter 13: Building Trust Is Essential

Trust is a driver and significant influence on our growth, it is omnipresent, without it our relationships will simply decline. It is reflected in how we work, the words we express and the actions we present. Without trust, collaboration falls apart quickly and, sometimes is irreparable. Being void of trust decreases reliability, it is so easy to trust blindly and have faith in others and fail to determine or establish mutual trust and understand ulterior motivations.

I reached out to Caroline Hayward, CEO, of The Chairman's Network an international network for Chairman's, Business owners and Leaders on her view of Trust and why it is important for business. Caroline provided a simple but striking statement, "Trust to me is a firm belief in the reliability, truth, or ability of someone or something" At the Chairman's Network, we are a "collaborative business network". We are bringing together Leaders in the UK and Internationally to connect, engage and do business together in a professional but informal way.

As far as I can see, driving your business is about collaborating with new pertinent individuals and companies to find and execute a win-win approach for all parties. In the dictionary, as above, it's about parties that "may not have any previous relationship" It's the relationship building and collaboration that creates the trust that leads to opportunities. If you don't invest that time, nothing will happen- much like all those extraneous contacts you have on LinkedIn. They probably won't come to anything.

Trust is so valuable; without it, we will live in an empty void of mayhem. It touches and affects everything. Success comes easily when trust is present – when it is not present it seems to dismantle efforts in a split second. What I have learned is that trust does not occur in a second, impressions form quicker than trust, it is an aspect which is earned over time, and is multi-dimensional in context, it reflects one's honesty, integrity, and values, bottom line it is experienced and felt through how you think and act, a broken trust system, ethos and actions simply leads to inefficiency and distaste.

Trust is a vital component of collaboration and driven by people and processes, on the people side, the four traits which distinguish trustworthy people are:

- Reliable: Peoples thoughts and guidance counts and are consistent.

- Authentic: Likable, humble and easy to talk to.

- Integrity: And have compassion.

- Empathetic: It's not all about them.

- How many of the above traits strike a chord with you?

Emotionally, trust exposes vulnerabilities: when we trust others, we open ourselves up to them with the belief that they will not take advantage of us. Trust has two dimensions: the emotional and the logical. The logical side is the rational assessment of probabilities, the emotional trust is defined as emotional security, or feeling secure, emotionally, it is where you expose your vulnerabilities to people.

Trust is something we bank now or in the future. We exchange it on the basis that there is a reciprocal arrangement that is fair and equitable. If this did not exist, then we would experience high levels of uncertainty in our dealings with others. We must learn to trust that we are making the right decision, we cannot experience distrust if we don't understand what trust is.

When we trust blindly, we leave ourselves and others exposed to be taken advantage of. This increases when we do not evaluate the vulnerabilities in ourselves and our teams. Brazen disrespect for trust leads to the temptation to abuse any exposed weaknesses. We trust that people will not cross into such voids of wisdom but, in truth, many projects and businesses fail because the elements of trust are diffused and taken advantage off.

Thus, trust is made up of three pillars: ability, sincerity, and history. Trust is about reliability and doing the right thing. It's also a major factor in determining success in all collaborative efforts, in your job and your career.

Trust is a characteristic that builds respect and loyalty, as well as a supportive and safe work environment. Distrust increases tension and negative, defensive behavior, which can erode the spirit of the team and ultimately productivity. Be consistent, honest, and balanced in judgment.

- Trust pillars provide stability to actions:

- Ability: Do they have the skill, knowledge, and tools to do the task?

- Sincerity: Do they have the desire, interest, and motivation to do the task?

- History: Is there a repetitive pattern? Are there examples that provide evidence to validate those trusting tendencies?

Of these three traits, Ability is multidimensional, sincerity is always subject to proof, and history will always leave some form of evidence. Each of these pillars are crucial, they provide stability when considered with the four traits described earlier.

Trust enables forward progress, preventing circular, non-action and fosters mutual accountability.

Remember trust is earnt through actions and time!

Chapter 14: Driving Innovation Forward

The context of innovation is well versed and often seeded in strategic dialogue; there will always be a requirement for new ideas, products, and opportunities, without it we would remain primitive in our thinking and living. It is not a given that by simply hiring the most talented and creative people that we can inspire new breakthroughs; we need to ensure we have a corresponding environment to allow ideas to germinate.

Make certain that a reliable, functional structure for floating ideas and acting on them is in place. Random brainstorming sessions without proper structure may be fun, but they are highly unlikely to bring any measurable results. Develop a set of techniques that will allow the best ideas to come to the surface, this adds structure to discussions and fosters unique and meaningful expression to grow.

My advice to leaders is that by allowing relationships to grow, we drive sustainable innovation. The interpersonal and community relationship within an organization should be considered just as important as finding the right party to collaborate with externally.

There are many stalwarts and gurus in the field of innovation. Within my own network, I have one such individual with whom I have collaborated quite a bit. His name is Dr. David Richards, and apart from being a friend, David is a leading strategist and was the co-founder of the MIT Innovation Lab. David has, over his career, created billions of dollars in shareholder value, broken into challenging markets, led change initiatives, driven digitalization, revitalized businesses, restored profitability, and achieved competitive leadership. Apart from his strategic lens, he is a qualified psychologist. In his book, he cites the importance of knowing how to get the most from people—inspiring, motivating and engaging in a highly collaborative, facilitative, and integrative way. Dr. Richards' book The Seven Sins of Innovation published by Palgrave, is well worth the read.

It's great when David and I meet; there are no egos at play, and we are at both at ease, intellectually inspiring each other. Some of my most inspirational dialogues are a result of those wonderful engagements with David. One of our recent encounters ended up with us collaborating on the fly.

We had a meeting and decided to test the power of unplanned thinking, seizing moments as they occur. It was a wonderful experience, sheer enjoyment, which ended up in a five-hour talking spree, during which we decided to explore the challenges of innovation.

We talked about the importance of innovation zoning and value creation. What I found interesting was the concept of building and considering those bridges where we must cross the important hard stuff of strategy and bottom line results in the soft stuff—psychology, mindset, motivations, and beliefs—and the organizational soup we call culture.

This bridge is not one, but many. We cross many of these bridges through collaboration and when forming synergies. We not only bridge the gaps, but we also stride from one bank of opportunity to another as well, and in the process, crisscross different contexts, people, and ideas. We must actively engage in the process of synergy development and evaluation during the process of value creation.

- Are you most creative from your normal day to routine?

- What bridges are the most important ones which you need to cross?

I believe that a huge portion of today's innovative ideas come not from large, established companies and corporations, but from small, often underfunded, startup companies. If the old saying "necessity is the mother of invention" can be shown to have validity it is surely here, among the individuals and small companies that must compete creatively to survive in a world dominated by large corporations. In their drive to effectively compete against the entrenched legacy systems and cumbersome infrastructure of major companies, these newer firms are disproving some long-held myths associated with innovation. I have come across two such myths which I would like to dispel.

Myth number one: Innovation starts at the top

All too often employees at all levels of a company come up with clever, time, and money-saving ideas only to find themselves ignored, or even actively ridiculed by their boss and general management. This is a perfect example of the failure of the old pyramid system, which believes that only the boss, or outside consultants, are capable of creative thought.

Both upper and middle management must realize that anyone, at any rung on the corporate ladder, can come up with ideas capable of saving or generating vast amounts of money, and can make a difference to a collaborative opportunity.

Indeed, management should encourage all its employees to work toward better, more efficient ways of doing things, and establish an atmosphere that engenders innovation. Great ideas can be nurtured. Some have established what is known as quick hits; a process focused on bringing immediate improvements to the day-to-day problems. The idea behind quick hits is that those who are closest to the problems are the most likely to come up with solutions that will make a difference. But it is also worthwhile to allow others to bring new perspectives from a broader team, which will reduce the influence of over-familiarity.

To bring in new perspectives, others are encouraged to bring their solution or ideas to the table. The institution of a quick hits program not only delivers real results to real problems, but it also demonstrates that you are committed to implementing the workforce's most promising ideas, be they large or small. A quick hits program covers idea generation through its execution and implementation.

Those directed with putting the quick hits program into operation should interview each member, asking them to offer ideas for solutions to everyday problems that could be implemented in less than ninety days, and would lead to increased production efficiency. Anyone wishing to submit an idea is asked to present it to the program's leadership team. If their idea is approved for implementation, the individual who submitted it will be given full credit for their creativity.

To have the greatest impact on morale, the implementation of ideas must take place relatively quickly—not only so the people suggesting the ideas know that their efforts are being instituted rather than shelved indefinitely, but also so that the beneficial effects of such ideas can be realized in the shortest possible time span. Swift implementation of new ideas will inevitably lead to the greatest level of support from the workforce, as each successfully applied idea encourages evermore creative levels of output.

Myth number two: Creativity and innovation is limited to the few

While creativity and innovation can be impressive forces, I have found through my engagements that some of the best innovations can come from anyone, and from anywhere. Creativity alone does not guarantee that innovation will succeed; for that to happen, it is essential that the ideas be executed in such a way that they produce meaningful results.

To remain productive and competitive, organizations engaged in businesses of every nature must learn to utilize innovation to focus on the challenges of their business or organization, regardless of size.

The process of innovation has many different aspects, and the people within an organization can play many different roles in bringing new ideas and ways of doing things into being. Some of us are dreamers: those of us whose minds are always looking to the future, seeking new, better, and more efficient ways of doing things. These are the people who can make connections that others miss. The dreamers are always asking "What if..." and "Why not..." It is this kind of thinking that leads to seeing opportunities long before anyone else even realizes there is a problem that needs addressing.

Others see innovation in a more immediate way than the dreamers. We call these people bright sparks. Bright sparks are the active, energetic people whose innovative power comes at unexpected times, in flashes of brilliance.

These people may be carrying out some seemingly mundane activity when they will suddenly see a new and better way of doing the job at hand faster and easier than ever before. A truly effective innovation team will include as many different types of creative minds, implementers, and collective thinkers as possible. A group of dreamers without individuals capable of implementing their dreams and turning them into reality is a sea of wasted talent and lost potential.

During my conversation with David. He explained that one of the key questions that leaders should ask is who they should consider partnering and collaborating with; not in the reduced passive form, but in the bold, why? It is when we frame those questions correctly that we establish clarity.

In closing this chapter, I ask you to consider the following questions:

1. Why should someone collaborate and partner with you?

2. Why is it important to create and innovate?

3. Why will intentions and creativity support the value exchange process?

While it may sometimes prove a challenge to convince others to take part in the process of collaborative creation, once the participation begins it may be just as difficult to get people to stop generating ideas and concentrate on the collaborative process of developing one idea into a workable format.

In such instances, the collaborative process is no longer the grease that reduces friction, but the sand that causes the machine to grind to a halt. To prevent such potential disasters, I have outlined a funneling process through which bold ideas move when they are created and implemented. It is quick and easy to apply.

Rapid ideation

Move from the first impulse to creative insight. This process is greatly enhanced by open dialogue among all those tasked with generating the idea.

Rapid sifting

Sort through ideas as quickly as they are proposed, and make determinations as to whether they are viable within the context of the existing business. Develop a scorecard that helps you to understand the relative value of each focus area.

Worthy of mention: The rapid sifting phase is often the one that gets lost in translation, as the saying goes. Great ideas are not difficult to generate. However, what is challenging is the evaluation of them regarding their strategic and or tactical impact.

How do you score ideas? What factors need to be considered? And how will you assess the benefit values relative to each other?

My advice is this: just as much as it is important to generate ideas, it is just as important to score them so that they can be sifted and therefore be assessed, prioritised and considered.

Rapid prototyping

Experiment as quickly as possible to discover if a given idea is viable. If an approach looks like it is going to be a failure, move on in the knowledge that subsequent approaches will bring better results.

Chapter 15: The Value Of Co-Creation

There will be times, when we can't innovate on our own, we may all have the same universe of knowledge available to us, and the challenges may be the same, trying to solve problems on our own, yields seldom appeasement. If over the course of the next decade, co-creation can live up to its promise, it will undoubtedly produce an explosive spawning of new concepts, business models and services and new forms of partnerships and innovations.

Co-creation is one of those terms that has generated a lot of buzz in recent years. Simply stated, co-creation is a method of innovation where the input is sought from all levels of an organization, as well as from abroad array of outside sources—all of which are aimed at achieving a specified goal. The range of groups and individuals who can be involved in the co-creative process is nearly limitless: from partnership development groups to strategic alliances, to input from individual customers. The co-creative process can take place in highly structured meetings, casual gatherings, or even online. As a result, co-creation offers nearly limitless possibilities to motivate, innovate, and create new and exciting approaches to personal and business growth, and it cuts across every department and end users or customers.

Co-creation will undoubtedly cause tremendous disruption to those who are familiar and comfortable with the traditional way of doing business. Along the way, there will unquestionably be a vast number of new elements thrown into the co-creative process, making the transition even more complicated. We can look forward to the coming together of varying groups in new and unexpected cooperative undertakings.

The key to the co-creative process is to keep all the various stakeholders focused on the goal of combining efforts that shape the desired outcome through a wide variety of forms of engagement. Considering the vast flexibility offered here, keeping everyone focused on a common goal will prove to be both exciting, and a distinct and unique challenge.

I should pause here and distinguish between co-production—which is the collaboration of different groups and individuals aiming to influence the product or service that a company offers—and value co-creation— which is an all-encompassing, complex and dynamic process in which the participants in the co-creative process determine the actual value of the product or service on which they are working. Simply put, co-production is an active component of the co-creation of value that represents the combined input of the firm and its customers on the firm's product or service.

In the co-creative process, collaborative leadership requires that all managers, heads of departments, and members of the board of directors understand, and are aligned with, the intrinsic value and benefits of the co-creative process, and set in place a program to support all aspects of the process. The sort of collaborative leadership as an essential anchor of contemporary corporate strategy.

Initiating the co-creative process will require a vast variety of skills, including the nurturing of relationships, the ability to visualize the desired outcome of the process, and the ability to impart this vision to others, all while having a firm grasp on both the business' current horizon and a variety of possible future horizons. As diverse perspectives begin to come into focus while the co-creative process unfolds, the collaborative leader will have to learn how to juggle various innovative insights, keep widely divergent efforts headed toward a coherent goal, and guarantee that the ongoing action leads toward the desired results. This balancing act will be vital, for the co-creative process to succeed in the creation of novel, groundbreaking experiences that have the potential to reshape individual and collective mindsets.

I recently caught up with Daniel Hulme, CEO of Satalia and TEDx Speaker, who is also the Director of Business Analytics MSc, at UCL and Advisor at the Home Office UK on AI & Ethics. University College London (UCL) is London's leading multidisciplinary university, currently ranked joint 7th in the QS World University Rankings. He holds an international Kauffman Global Entrepreneur Scholarship, and actively promotes entrepreneurship and technology innovation across the globe.

Satalia is a spin-out venture of UCL that provides a unique artificial intelligence technology and professional services to solve industry's most robust problems. Daniel is passionate about emerging technology and regularly speaks at events with interests in algorithms, optimization, analytics, big data, artificial intelligence, organizational structure, innovation, entrepreneurship, philosophy, ethics, and the future internet.

When I met Daniel, I was instantly taken aback by his deep understanding of co-creation. He did not just talk about it; he demonstrated his willingness to engage; a glimpse of the Satalia website outlines this under the Ethos heading.

Human

We love people and hate politics.

By caring for one another's wellbeing, we increase our relatedness and reduce the inefficiencies of company politics.

Expert

We improve collaboratively.

Our expertise is cultivated as much through the concerted and sustained efforts of our teams, as it is through our individual progression.

Adaptive

We learn quickly and iterate.

Problem-solving is most effective when we use lean thinking and agile methods to innovate, measure and iterate our way to solutions.

What do you find striking about the above?

I asked Daniel, "How does collaboration influence your world?" He expressed the following: "IT development is rapidly becoming redundant in the new world of easily accessible AI-based software services and solutions. Existential threats to well-established business models come from indirect competitors with massive investment into data-driven operations.

Co-created solutions provide complete control, allowing for agile solutions that operationalize tacit domain knowledge, and rapidly adapt to changing markets.

The above statement highlights the importance given to co-creation. The inclusion of customers and value chain contributors in the co-creative process emphasizes the importance of the ultimate user in the creative process and indicates that businesses should pay greater attention to their customers, involving them in the innovation process.

The enthusiasm and dedication of the large number and broad range of individuals who are likely to be involved in a co-creative team will be significantly enhanced and encouraged if an initiating team oversees the group.

Are you someone who is naturally inclusive or are you exclusive?

Chapter 16: Thinking And Questioning

Hidden among the vast array of odd bits of information, experiences, and accrued wisdom that each of us collects over the course of our lifetime are thoughts and ideas that have the potential to be of great value. Each of us is a font of untapped wisdom, just waiting to be released...if only we can learn how to tap into it.

Many fail to understand that collaborative group efforts lubricate the wheels of progress. They can, in just as many instances, be the sand that brings progress to a grinding halt. When a company becomes overly reliant on ineffective teams, the principles of collaboration become blocked by inefficiency, and the only result is a string of endless meetings in which ideas are debated, and consensus continually fades into the horizon. We see this all too often in a corporate culture, where the only positive thing ever said is "Let's take a meeting." Is this something you have experienced?

How do we begin to sort through the staggering amount of information and input that each of us receives every day, and file it neatly away so that we can access it when we need to? And why are some people so much better at doing this than others?

I found an interesting perspective from Justin Moore, Chief Sales Officer at City Sprint. I asked Justin why some people miss valuable opportunities and do not seize moments, but others see and seize them. His response was "This question bedevils me daily. I guess motivation is a factor, alongside the ability to turn dialogue into opportunity".

How would you answer the question? What does Justin's response reveal to you?

One of the questions we must answer is: do we all pick up the same clues and signals as everyone else? Do three people process information the same way? The answer is no; they do not. Even when people perceive a given event or need in the same way, they may not process it the same way, because some people have been indoctrinated into a conformist mindset by society, peer groups, political views of the world, or culture of the business for which we work and others will be activists and march forward come what may.

Creative adaptation of existing information is far more likely to occur in an individual who has a naturally creative mindset, is by nature a non-conformist, or has trained themselves to look at the world from a slightly different angle than most their peer group.

It is equally valid that where one person sees potential benefit and value in a certain way, another person will also see benefit and value—but they will perceive it in an entirely different way, or envision it applied to a radically different end. The value of collaborative cooperation is enhanced when various and diverse perspectives come together in such a way that the result meets the expectations and goals of all concerned and generates impact. Achieving this end can be a long, arduous and often frustrating process. Do not allow yourself to become disillusioned in the process. Continue to ask the bold questions and offer equally bold solutions; in perseverance lies the pathway to success.

In some cases, innovation can be spurred by a seemingly unreasonable demand, like a strict time frame, or a reasonable demand with unforeseen constraints. Even if we manage to come up with a viable solution, it may be rejected out of hand for no greater reason than the fact that we did not frame it correctly. Such things are less likely to happen if we put forth our expectations to be met within a reasonable period, and offer support rather than criticism—but this does not always happen.

Because of all these possible hurdles, we may not reach our desired goal during the prescribed time allotted to the project, and only later come up with what seems like an obvious solution. Some people beat themselves up over their failure to come up with the right answer at the right time. Unfortunately, we are not machines. We are limited, and we should accept that we cannot always perform on cue.

A lot of ideas that cause major upheavals are painfully obvious in retrospect. Simple ideas have connected and created global platforms and spawned new engagement models. Anyone of us could have come up with any of these ideas, but it was someone else who did. Do not be discouraged. Some things take far longer than seems reasonable before they happen. Consider that we put a man on the moon twenty years before anyone thought of putting wheels on a suitcase.

Everything will come in its own time, including your next great idea. Until your next flash of inspiration comes, here are some questions to reflect on.

1. Are you the sort of the person who can spot opportunities easily?

2. How do you sift through those ideas?

3. What criteria do you use to filter them?

4. When was the last time you had an excellent idea?

5. Do you seize moments, or let them flit by?

In a very real sense, success relies on many aspects. One of them is thinking outside of the box, and another is the courage to ask bold questions. It can be uncomfortable, but if we do not ask questions that challenge us and others, we end up being complacent, masking our avoidance by scurrying from place to place, never stopping to engage in self-reflection. Bold questions challenge us and may lead us to move in entirely new, often unexpected directions. Only by seeking out the new and novel can we discover the best path.

Asking bold questions of ourselves and others will ignite a greater sense of curiosity, which can force us to ask even more questions and make inquiries into new fields of expertise. Bold questions lead to learning new things. Examining new ideas and adopting new modes of thought yields new approaches to value and collaborative modeling come into existence. An experimental approach to questions, going beyond the simple yes/no scenario and delving into the collaborative concept of exploring through real interest, can be especially useful when you are dealing with stakeholders untrained in systems thinking.

I have always been an advocate of challenging ourselves with those difficult but constructive questions that can lead us toward new ways of seeing things.

Here is a list of questions that every bold thinker should ask themselves on a regular basis:

1. What is the next big idea?

2. What prevents you from acting on it?

3. Why do some organizational structures fail when others succeed?

4. How do we unlock the passions and talents within each of us?

5. What prevents you from achieving your goals?

6. What innovations might lead to significant advancements?

7. How can we best integrate efforts that are simultaneously strategic, opportunistic, and responsive?

8. If you had an ability fund, what would you place in it?

9. What does success look and feel like?

10. What is your purpose?

Michael Boulton, Strategy Director of Whistl, a leading value-added postal services company in the UK, highlights the strength and power of one question, which he uses when developing strategic blueprints: Why?! It was only when he said it that it dawned on me; he has a point. It's one of those questions you can't fudge a response to. It leaves you exposed if you do; yet, when answered clearly, understanding surges forward.

Many times, we begin viewing our situations, goals, and life through the lens that things are overwhelming; we're too busy, or it's all just plain hard to fathom. We will question, but still be unable to unearth the answer we seek. Perhaps this is because we may be positioning and framing questions in the wrong context. Let's use two different types of questions to illustrate this, what versus why.

"What are you grateful for today?" vs. "Why are you grateful?"

Which question is easier to answer? Which one leaves you exposed, if you get your reply wrong? Why is much more difficult to answer, as it requires you to think and go beyond a recall response. It is one of those questions Boulton asks more than any other, to get a complete understanding.

What are some of the why questions you can ask?

- Why is this important to you?

- Why have you made that decision?

- Why do you feel that way?

- Why do you want to make a change?

Michael deepens his reasoning by stating that these questions have a certain quality; it generates energy and momentum. It is capable of:

- Generating more answers.

- Requiring you to stir the creative pot to provide an answer.

- Creating a climate of exploration, because it has a degree of quality to it.

- Revealing underlying assumptions.

It is not just the question itself which counts; it is also how it is expressed. I would strongly suggest that we take note of Michael's point of reference. It is truly revealing and has substance beyond the occasional use. The next time you need clarity, frame this power question well; it will yield tremendous value.

How will you develop better questions and listening skills?

Chapter 17: Using Collaboration To Grow Relationships

When we form strong bonds with people with whom we are in a dialogue with, we build credibility, respect and trust which supports our chances of gaining commitment and closing opportunities, quickly and more reliability. The sharing and emphasis of value become important, which is encouraged by the willingness of both parties to trust and respect the intents and opportunities of both sides of the dialogue.

Here are four steps to engage others:

Prepare to collaborate: When you engage others, the idea is to invite them to be an active participant in a process, not someone who listens and who does not contribute.

Inspire insights: Foster dialogue which creates those "Ah ha moments to flow, resulting in high-level sparks of wonder to take hold. When buyers answer your questions, you can share stories of how the problems they see have been solved at other places. You can also guide them by saying, for example, "Let's look at that last roadblock" and consider how we could have worked through it and how to work through the next one. It is through the power of collaborative conversation that problematic barriers can be overcome.

Ask incisive questions: Bold questions if relevant and timely, set a tone that you understand and are interested, by defining the agenda, the scope and levels of interest are advocated through agreement. I mentioned being timely. There is little value in asking bold questions with no relevance, it signals you are not prepared and not in control, it breathes discomfort and creates tension.

Shape discussions mutually: It is through involvement that we shape solutions. When relationships bond, we also drive commitment to through self-acceptance. It is harder to break a commitment when both parties have already confidently planted seeds in their collective future.

Collaborative dialogue is the mindset of cooperation through ensuring a win/win of joint efforts. Where relationships not only form but build strength and perform.

What's your process of building relationships?

Chapter 18: Changes Are Occurring In All Sectors Globally

Today we are standing on the cusp of changes in technology and emerging innovations, and business relationships are shifting as we adapt to rapidly changing market demands. The emergence of new economies has ushered in imminent business opportunities for many organizations, both private and public, those who commit to collaborate will emerge as winners.

Collaboration is both a process, which occurs through a result of the synthesis of a series of events. Although collaboration is easy to conceptualize and discuss, it can be difficult to put into practice in some high-pressure environments. I believe that part of this difficulty comes about because of barriers to the sharing large amounts of critical information, combined with job pressure and the skills necessary to institute a shared environment, all of which takes time to get accustomed to.

We are seeing tremendous growth in the collaborative/shared economy as co-dependent platforms bring people and services together quickly and easily, a reduction in business and operational friction and the maximization of shared resources provides scale and efficiency leverage. To me, efficiency represents the degree to which resources are used to generate productive outcomes. In other words, the greatest possible bang for one's buck.

Wealth management

I recently caught up with Rohit Sarin, founder of India's largest multifamily office, Client Associates. I threw this question on the table: How do trust and collaboration intersect what you do? Here is what he had to say: "A single-minded, client-centric approach guided the foundation of Client Associates. It began with the name itself. Then its practice model was built around the very needs of a client. CA's unique selling point is that it manages the entire financial affairs of their clients. In other words, a Private Banker at Client Associates is the Chief Financial Officer, or CFO, for his client".

Today, Client Associates is recognized by private clients and the industry at large as not only the pioneers of the family office firm in India but also as one of the best teams of private bankers in India. Its 20 plus private bankers work very closely with over 450 wealthy families and private institutions of India.

Trust and collaboration are the two fundamentals upon which Client Associates has been built during its journey of 15 years. In an intensely hyper-competitive market like India, it isn't easy to build anything that matters. Having chosen to grow organically from starting out as India's first multi-family office (MFO) firm to the largest MFO in the country required more than just entrepreneurial passion, it required the DNA and values that constitute the true personality of an MFO. As a business model, an MFO is supposed to be a client-centric platform, representing the client's interests and doing anything and everything that a client would like to do for his wealth, but doesn't have the time. It is supposed to function like a client's private office.

The conceptual construct of an MFO can't work without deep trust between itself and the client. While trust is the first step, an MFO can't deliver on the mandate without delivery capabilities across multiple domains, which many times could be specializations in disciplines such as taxation, legal, investment banking, succession planning, direct investing, cross-border investing, etc. This required building long-term partnerships and collaborations involving partners with proven strengths in their respective specialist domains.

We built trust on the foundation of two principles: complete transparency in relationships, and ensuring alignment of interests in any relationship. Our goals were wholly aligned with those of our customers and partners. It required us to follow an open architecture model of not manufacturing any in-house products, which has allowed us to retain our independence to date.

Collaborations have been built over the years with the spirit of never saying no to solving a client's problem. In our quest for finding solutions for our clients, we have built deep domain partnerships with like-minded partners in different specialist domains beyond the core domain of investment management.

What is clear is that Client Associates has built significant trust-based relationships and deepened them through multi-disciplinary focus, personalization and relationship stickiness. This bond enables Client Associates to pursue its larger purpose: leaving the world richer than we inherited it.

Furthering Rohit's comments - I have found that it is the strength of synergy which binds and drives growth. Think about all those great established networks we engage with or have heard of, not just in business, but in the social segment. It would be hard for me to list them all, and if I did, I am sure I would need a separate book to cover them all. Some of these networks are significant in what they do, with thousands of members, united to make a difference - think of the United Nations, the Junior Chambers International, and the Lions Club, The Drucker Foundation, The Association of Strategic Alliance Professionals, The Institute of Directors and the portfolio of Chartered professional bodies, whose structures and mandates co-exist with members who provide the tremendous goodwill so that a value exchange flows. These organizations touch upon the lives of millions of people around the world, with far-reaching, impacts at a social and economic level.

Supply chains

The process of enhancing social and economic development by providing better value and establishing more functional value chains is a fundamental component of any thriving economy. Examining these factors should give us an insight into significant economic shifts that are yet to come. This is especially important in the case of the supply chain because it is always changing.

I foresee significant growth in the efficient use of assets (both existing and yet to be constructed), initiating shared distribution centers and city hub supply systems, utilizing alternative forms of energy and enacting joint logistics solutions. These will reduce the cost of doing business, and add value for the customer.

As market forces change, the supply chain's many moving components, like people, systems, and interactions can be caught in bottlenecks which stifle efficiency and demand change. To stay ahead will require us to establish a remedy to solve such challenge; the solution is contained within structured relationships and enhanced communication, (aka collaboration) across the value chain.

Even today, new and innovative generations of supply chains are being developed and put into action. These revolutionary systems are no longer simple reactions to market demand; they are proactive and are incorporating high-end technologies which can predict emerging patterns of demand before they happen. Such supply chains are undoubtedly being reshaped by the internet and developing trends in e-businesses, but there may also be other factors involved in their emergence.

In the UK—as is true in nearly all countries, both developed and developing—governmental bills are being drafted with the aim of substantially reducing the nation's carbon dioxide emissions by 2050. In some nations, this same problem has been addressed by establishing rigorous automotive emissions standards. Whatever options each nation has chosen to deal with the climate change problem, the results will mean significant shifts in how supply chains operate.

Thus, to some extent at least, we can project what form these changes are likely to take. Methods of distribution, warehousing, and infrastructure models will be forced to change. Companies will begin to share more infrastructure and services to consume less energy. But such supply chain collaboration can only exist if there is sufficient sharing of information, this may see the growth of more vendor-neutral agnostic platforms being built to help optimize and drive new synergies with different components of the supply-demand ecosystem.

Professor Tom Cherrett, University of Southampton, and Julian Allen, University of Westminster (both leading research projects into supply chain collaboration) mutually issued this statement:

"Collaboration between organizations working in supply chains has a major influence on shaping corporate strategy and putting in place efficient and cost-effective logistics operations. It also has a vital role to play in bringing about freight transport activities that are more sustainable from a traffic and environmental perspective. Some organizations have already begun to experiment with supply chain collaboration and the results, for both these companies and for wider society and the planet, are impressive."

My view is that there will be an inherent requirement for a higher level of informational transparency; there will be an increased demand by consumers to know how their shopping choices will impact the drive toward sustainability. Already, the vastly increased tendency to shop online has had a noticeable impact on how much time people spend on shopping excursions, and hence, on business in brick-and-mortar stores. As shopping and e commerce patterns change, online shops will flourish, driving demand for greater home delivery. Some individual retail stores and even some major chains will be required to find new ways to compete—or face bankruptcy and closure. The coming change will be consumer-driven, but it will impact virtually every segment of the retail and logistics markets.

The world of commerce no longer has the option of taking a wait-and-see attitude. These changes are already underway, whether we like it or not. If businesses do not learn to adapt now, they will be in for a nasty surprise in the very near future. The market is already being reshaped, based on technical and socioeconomic factors; the future well-being of businesses and industries worth trillions of dollars in combined revenues are already beginning to change.

The new challenges that the industry is facing will necessitate the implementation of new and creative types of supply chains, and industry needs to immediately begin devising innovative ways to support the dynamic flux of customer demands.

Developing this new kind of supply chain will require time and creative insight to design, and once a plan has been devised, additional time to implement. Input will be required from a broad variety of sources, including retailers, consumers, distributors, product manufacturers, industry standards organizations, and technology companies. Such groups will be able to achieve their goals with far greater efficiency and speed if they have a working understanding of how the collaborative team approach will smooth their path, and move the planning process ahead with the greatest possible speed and efficiency.

For the enhanced collaboration process to work effectively, the participants must re-evaluate and improve their existing concepts of collaboration. Just as the collaborative process itself will provide greater efficiency and an improved supply chain, so a re-evaluation of their existing mode of cooperating and communicating ideas will bring greater efficiency to the collaborative process. This collaborative approach can be shared between manufacturers and could be expanded to logistics providers, to make transportation more efficient through every step of the process, from moving raw materials to home delivery. Ultimately, this effort will result in a vastly more physically and economically efficient supply chain, with improvements in efficiency, cost advantages, information sharing, warehousing, and delivery systems.

Collaborative supply chains will eventually become the norm as fierce competition, limited resources, and ecological necessity combine to bring information technology to the forefront as a tool in the process to provide ever greater efficiency, and profit created through the proper use of limited resources.

Future supply chains will need to be based on models that can support multi-partner information sharing among all stakeholders. Those who insist on clinging to existing, outmoded supply chains will find themselves left behind as these changes take place— and their profits will decrease commensurately.

As is true with supply chains, the efficacy of collaborative, sustainable transport efforts will be an essential part of a more efficient overall approach to doing business. The effectiveness of these transportation and delivery systems will be measured in the expenditure of fewer and more economical miles. This goal can be achieved through a more efficient approach to assets, such as green buildings and more fuel-efficient transport vehicles. Collaborations of stakeholders must also make use of regional consolidation centers, as well as co-managed logistics hubs.

Under this new model, outlying warehouse locations could become shared cross-docking locations, where final mile delivery takes place through consolidated warehouse facilities, as well as co-shared, cooperated, or co-managed city delivery systems. Sharing infrastructure, such as warehouse storage and transportation vehicles, to simplify and reduce the physical footprint of all those involved will provide efficiency of both time and resources, as well as serving as a green-friendly solution to ecological concerns.

The most costly and challenging part of transportation is the final delivery from city hubs to the ultimate consumer's home or business. In this most fragmented part of the chain, new technologies, platforms, and crowd-sharing solutions will come into play. This will provide an opportunity for new startups to collaborate with more established players and complement their existing services. Last mile services will encourage new technologies to grow as city hubs become shared resources that generate extra revenue through consolidation of costs and resources.

Sharing and collaboration can take place both between and across various types of competitive supply chains and can be applied to both existing infrastructure and new, purpose-built collaborative networks.

Recruitment

Globally, the recruitment sector is worth billions. It is the one area that impacts each of us at some stage of our career, in some form or another. It's one of those sectors that will see a tremendous change in the next five years. The process of recruitment involves several processes and systems that include human and IT-supported decisions, based on a broad range of data points and information.

As businesses become agiler, borders change, customer segments emerge, companies will face several challenges, such as social and technological changes, cultural diversity, aging populations, and political instability. This is on top of skills shortages, dwindling talent pools, and skill gaps. A consequence of this is that there is an ever-increasing focus on effective recruitment.

The recruitment landscape is an entirely different beast than it was twenty, or even ten years ago. Recruiters will need to be more proactive as competition increases. Recruiters have the responsibility now to look for not just amicable personalities and hard workers, but those with high potential for synergy. Collaboration reinforces unity and builds a culture of feedback, transparency, and everyone feeling valued. People on your team will know that they have a voice and are an important part of the vision you're all working toward. Think about it, who doesn't want an awesome work culture?

I see tremendous value and growth in the use of AI and machine learning, and thus, consistency will improve; all those unstructured data points we have will be understood in a nanosecond, consistently and evenly. This will reshape industry as we know it, and although human interaction will still be necessary, a closer collaboration with technological innovation will be required. This is one sector in which I foresee the next disruptor as having a chance to create truly inspiring collaborative platforms.

Several key factors will drive this change, they include:

Recruiters want to cut through the chaff and get to the quality candidates. But many excellent candidates are missed because current processes and systems fail to spot those hidden talents and gems. As technologies evolve and are proven, they will disrupt the process and offer a tremendously different experience than is currently available.

For every person eventually placed in a role, hundreds seem to get lost in the process—even though it is supposed to be people friendly. Surely, there are opportunities which can address this in more connected manner.

The biggest opportunity here is clear: the candidate-recruiter collaboration, engagement model, predictive intelligence, talent exploration, breaking down of suitability through analysis of much more wider and broader data points, and the use of much more personalized technology will all create a much more user-friendly experience.

Here are some questions to consider: if you looked at your endorsements on your social profile, what do they represent, what's the message, which groups of people seem to provide you valuable commendations? This is just one example of how simple data points overall portray certain images.

Healthcare

Establishing and managing a collaborative team is one of those things that are much easier to talk about than enact. This is especially true in the highly pressurized and varied hierarchical environment of clinical and patient care.

In the realm of healthcare, collaboration is defined in one of two ways: As a group of industry professionals assuming complementary roles and working together in a cooperative setting, or alternatively, as a group of technologists and researchers joining forces to drive innovation. In either case, the collaboration will result in a sharing of responsibility for a strategic approach to problem-solving and innovation.

In the healthcare industry, the most important priorities are patient care, research, and administration. All three of these factors are time intensive, and this allows little time for establishing and maintaining collaborative teams. Consequently, when a healthcare facility does engage in forming a collaborative team, they may not have a chance to communicate efficiently; thus, the collaborative effort may fail, and patient care and safety can be put at risk.

Even during a stay of only a few days, a patient will interact with physicians, nurses, technicians, dieticians, and possibly clinical pharmacists and surgeons; it requires a high degree of collaboration among this widely varied group of people to guarantee that all necessary information is shared among everyone who needs it to guarantee the patient's well-being. While team collaboration is always characterized by common purpose, adherence to behavioral standards, trust, and respect in any situation, it is quite literally a matter of life and death in the healthcare industry.

This demand for close collaboration requires a high level of dedication and a willingness to address every new situation as it occurs, on a minute-by-minute basis. I was speaking with a close friend recently, who is training to be a vascular technologist, Meena Archibald, who recently took a complete career change to serve those in need. What I found amazing was the passion she had, which struck me, and the sincerity she brings to her work in trying to help people. Conjuring up an admirable relationship with surgeons and patients alike, each with their own mindsets, the surgeon wanting to help, the patient in a state of apprehension. It was the explanation of her role that struck home importance of empathy and emotional intelligence.

Anyone who has visited a health clinic or hospital will understand very quickly the difference between a good and an excellent experience. There is nothing worse than systems failing, or inconsistencies of information, or that feeling that no one cares.

During my recent discussion with Noor Hasmat Ali the Director of a Family First Fostering a professional independent fostering agency (IFA) in the UK, Noor explained that he has a responsibility to ensure that all children who are supported, are carefully matched to the foster parents. Collaboration is key to the duty of care. It does not stop once the child is placed with a caring family, it extends to when children leave the bonds they have formed. Noor explains that we must ensure children, parents, and families are happy. It is not a tick box exercise. We impact lives and, as such, are responsible for making sure that everyone is happy. By supporting our careers, a better quality of care is provided to the children and young people.

Collaboration extends externally. There is value in community-based approaches, which encourages young people to interact with the outside world in an effort to ease their eventual transition to independent living. We continually strive to give new foster parents the skills and confidence they need when they choose to support a vulnerable child or young person in their home.

What strikes you the most in terms of the pressures which healthcare professionals have to deal with? In business and government, how do we cope compared to those who are healthcare professionals?

Government

Jane Otoka, who is currently the assistant director of information communication technology (ICT) of the Kenyan government, highlights her views on the importance of collaboration across the public-private spectrum.

In terms of collaborations between governments and citizens:

For governments to achieve targets that aim to endear the citizens to them, for the citizens to carry that vision/target, and sustain it (vision/target) by passing on the principles, which include a need for:

- Creating and sustaining trust among the citizens by government.

- Building capacity within the citizenry.

- Finding effective communication channels.

- Having an attitude change of both governmental officials and citizens.

- Encouraging commitment by both parties.

Collaboration within government:

- Supporting the need for champions of collaboration.

- Having think-tank capacity and proper planning.

- Building leadership from the top with the ability to rally to a vision.

- Encouraging ways to redefine/retrain/re-skill/retool.

- Ensuring attitude change/personal development.

- Honoring commitment.

- Assisting in simplifying complexities.

- Re-evaluating communication.

- Collaboration with external parties:

- Look at problems/solutions from various and diverse perspectives (together with external parties).

- Facilitate innovation processes/adoption/ mainstreaming of new solutions/technologies.

- Looking at motivations behind actions (patriotism, development, etc).

- Recognizing points of weakness and how other parties can fill in those gaps.

What I find striking about Jane's summary is the thread of synergies that cut across both public and private arenas. I have been fortunate enough to visit Kenya several times, having spoken at a range of events there while also interacting with government officials who have outlined their national transformation blueprints.

My experience is that the traits Jane has outlined are in the process of being embedded across several governmental bodies. It is through this type of collective approach that major change occurs.

What do you find striking about Jane's synopsis?

I believe that there are tremendous scopes for value chain improvement and co-creation that could have a significant transformational impact. But who are the collaboration influencers, and what can be done, so that information and breakthroughs are shared, not just locally, but regionally and globally as well? If you are looking for an international standard, one which would provide a broad but structured framework, check out ISO 44001, the first international collaborative business standard, which helps large and small organizations, in both public and private sectors, build and develop effective competitive business relationships based on a collaborative approach.

If you are engaged in collaborative dialogue within the public sector, what are the areas that strike you as needing an overhaul?

- How do you move beyond cooperation to collaboration across government entities?

- How would a framework help you create greater momentum internally?

If you are interested in learning more about Collaborative Leadership and ISO 44001 you may find resources available at https://shop.bsigroup.com/BSISO4400

Startups

To guide a startup business effectively, today's entrepreneurs need to understand the art of collaboration. Knowing how to work with established companies, as well as other startups, can help new ventures avoid the bureaucratic complications that often hamper larger firms. Not only can small startups benefit from collaborating with larger, more established firms, the large, existing firms can benefit at least as much from a liaison with their smaller counterparts.

There is a long-standing animus between the old boys of business and their up-and-coming counterparts. Established companies see startups as immediate threats that must be destroyed or absorbed. Consequently, small, new businesses historically view large firms as an immediate threat to their continued existence. While there is historical truth to both views, the fact is that neither of them is based on practicality or necessity.

By carefully instituting the right partnership arrangement, sometimes we mix the personality up with the character traits of those we engage with, only to unravel a complete difference of opinion, tension rises and falls out occur. Great relationships which allow synergy to flow provide fertile ground for entities to flourish to a far greater extent than either of them can on their own. Thus, they can become more efficient and create greater value for their customers and stockholders. Large, existing firms can offer protection and financial security to smaller companies, and new, young firms can provide their larger partners with the innovative mindset and agility to adapt to and compete in emerging sectors of the market.

Procuring services or products from startups can provide significant benefits to larger, established partner corporations by giving them access to cutting-edge technologies, new opportunities, and new business models. Such an arrangement will require a collaborative mindset, which supports the wholesale realignment of innovative value. Benefits for the startup include the validation of having a large corporation as a lead customer, an advantage which can often prove to be the tipping point between remaining small or scaling up, possibly even making the difference between success and failure.

Large, established businesses can also reposition themselves as being up to date, and innovation is driven by partnering with a pioneering startup. Such a partnership can assist in securing new customers and future employees, as well as modifying the public perception of the company.

Not least, the infusion of new ideas and new ways of doing things can alter internal corporate thinking along new and more innovative lines. From a purely economic standpoint, partnering with a startup can often be a money-saving way to improve on existing products, expand into new markets, develop new products, and find innovative solutions to new challenges. Such a partnership can help an existing company capture the power of cutting-edge ideas and technology.

Collaborative development of new products or services may include joint research and development programs that will benefit the corporation, their clients, or both. Such cooperative undertakings should be jointly specified, developed, and then piloted. The success of co-development typically depends on the development of a clear project brief, which initially emanates from the corporation—but is agreed to by both parties, has a pre-designated budget, and a clear time frame in which to decide whether to terminate the partnership after the project has ended, or retain the partnership structure and progress into additional new ventures.

The big questions include

1. How best can we expand into emerging markets?

2. How can we capture the power of cutting-edge technology?

3. How do we make our organization more innovative?

4. How can we solve critical business problems more quickly and cost-efficiently?

5. How do we create awareness of new market trends and emerging technologies?

How is your sector changing and what impact does it have on you

Chapter 19: Networking Is Vital

The effectiveness of our networks serves as a barometer of our ability to make effective connections, which drive new solutions, ideas, or value. The broader and more effective your network, the more knowledge you can tap into. Today's business world is all about connectivity, and we can harness the greatest possible amount of interactions while deriving some form of value and benefit.

The premise behind creating a synergistic atmosphere among members of the collaborative groups is to encourage relationships. What follows is the exploitation of similarities and dissimilarities. But, how many people are truly comfortable reaching out and engaging with people they have never met before, is the tendency to stand in one place rather than use the kinetic of intent to move and meet people and to share and explore?

But, for all the possible benefits it offers, networking can become a personal nightmare for those who cannot relax and adapt to the process. From the most outgoing to the most withdrawn, the broad spectrum of personality types that will inevitably be included in any team, moods, and contributions will swing like a pendulum.

Networking will unquestionably deliver a greater return, both monetarily and non-monetarily. The benefits of effective networking are broad and varied, and the larger your network grows, the more opportunities you will discover for expanding it even more. The larger your network, the more opportunities there are to generate increased referrals. Networking provides an abundance of potential, especially when done well. But effective networking involves more than smiling and handshaking. You must learn to understand, connect, explore, engage, and interact far beyond cursory greetings and farewells. Far too often, people fall over because they are uncomfortable stepping out of their comfort zone. The question is, why?

During the networking process, you become your own most important product. As we know, people buy people; the question is, are people drawn to your product? By effectively presenting yourself and the company you represent, you will raise your social and business profile and find that new and exciting opportunities will begin to come your way.

If you're looking at joining established networks check out The Chairman's Network which is a high level senior leadership network, members join to make a difference, (www.chairmansnetwork.com) and CEO Space (www.ceospaceinternational.com) a serious and major influencer in networking to grow. CEO Space is a network where business is done with like-minded people who join to do business, plus are mentored by some of the biggest and brightest minds in the business world. From financing and marketing to strategy and business law, their educators come from a variety of fields to share their expertise exclusively with enrollees and members.

So, what is the best way to implement an effective networking program in such a way that it will provide the greatest benefit to you, the company you represent, and to any prospective business contacts, be they those who are interested in collaboration or potential customers? The list below should provide a reliable set of preparation guidelines:

Know your target: Learn as much as you can about the people from outside your group with whom you will be dealing with. How much do you have in common? What are the points of interest you share? Are your values and goals akin? What problems are they facing now, and what solutions might you be able to offer that will help solve their problems? When you know your audience, it is easier to strike up a great conversation.

Stay current: Your pitch to both team members and those outside your group should never remain static. Think about all those reused decks, presentations, and opening one-liners that have in truth become stale. Are your presentational materials current? Never rely on content that is out of date; it is a trust breaker.

Frame your introduction: When encountering new people, either in groups or on a one-on-one level, always remember that first impressions count. Everything from the welcome and the initial handshake to your opening statements will set the tone for the rest of the meeting, determining whether your target audience will accept or reject you and your message. First impressions count, so make sure you stand out and make the encounter a memorable experience.

My view is that just as people are drawn to you when you put forth your best qualities, showing a deep personal interest in them is at least equally effective. Successful networkers are those who can form strong personal bonds, do the most they can to help one another and fulfill each other's needs, and know that with helping others comes to a great sense of satisfaction and personal accomplishment. It is what I call the Sea of Resonation: It's where efforts build momentum and waves of goodwill start to flow, one after the other; the emotions reach you, and it's a wonderful, pleasant feeling. Everything just seems to work in your favor.

We build great bonds not only when we connect intellectually, but socially as well. Sure, there will be different points of interest, but at an emotional level, there is a widespread interplay. We will all be influenced by intelligence, or by our own feelings or others' emotions. In fact, we need to understand the context of emotional intelligence within the minds of collaboration. I say this because we need to go beyond one person, to many. As with those tides of goodwill, we must manage different people and a range of different emotional banks. Some are stronger than others; every now and then, you will get one of those riptides, coming along to pull you out of your comfort zone. If you have not read about the influence that emotional intelligence has on your progress, then I would strongly recommend that you do a quick internet search to help internalize its importance.

I particularly refer to the work done by Daniel Goleman, who frequently lectures to audiences around the world. Goleman is a psychologist who, for many years, reported on the brain and behavioral sciences for The New York Times. One of his best-known works, Emotional Intelligence (Bantam Books), was on The New York Times bestseller list for a year and a half. It has been a best seller throughout Europe, Asia, and Latin America, and has been translated into forty languages. The book puts across the argument that human competencies like self-awareness, self-regulation, and empathy add value to cognitive abilities in many domains of life, from workplace effectiveness and leadership to health and relationships.

My reading of this extraordinary volume many years ago, and subsequently interacting occasionally with Daniel, has been hugely motivational. This has driven my self-confidence and shown me that when our intentions are placed well, we will resonate with people from all walks of life and backgrounds. It is through these interactions that I poise my skills to help others connect with global influencers.

There is another type of intelligence, which Daniel further expounds on, that also shapes our future. Daniel outlines the importance of social intelligence: complex socialization such as politics, romance, family relationships, quarrels, collaboration, reciprocity, and altruism drove the development of the human brain, and help us use our complex minds now.

He makes draws reference to the position of this important point against general IQ, examining the relationship between neuroscience and human interactions. Goleman finds that we are "wired to connect," and examines the impact that personal relationships have in every aspect of our lives.

Goleman defines social intelligence as being knowledgeable about both our interpersonal relationships and in how we act in them. He makes it a point to distinguish between self-serving and genuine acts of caring. Goleman uses his own research and life experiences, as well as the research, life experiences, and anecdotal evidence of others, to continually make his point about the impact our social and private relationships have on our lives.

Do you know how to unlock your network?

Chapter 20: Connect With Your Audience

We must seed and articulate our ideas in such a way that others buy into them, and the barriers which distort information flow is reduced. Connectivity is hence crucial. Honing your pitch to a razor-sharp edge is an essential part of your toolkit. No amount of skill can overcome the inertia of an entirely dead and unreceptive audience, but a well-rehearsed presentation can make even a moderately attentive audience sit up and take notice of you, and by extension, of what you are saying.

When arranging the group, it is essential to establish the correct collaborative dialogue, which the team can emulate. When a team breaks down into factionalism, it is almost always because the team leader was unable to staunch a small problem before it became a major, destructive force.

The more people we can bring into this process, the more value and good we can create and accomplish. Encouragement of continuing, regular, open communication is vital if collaborative efforts are to be sustained and progress is to be made toward desired goals. Continued communication allows interpersonal relationships to grow, enhancing the chance of a swift and decisive resolution to the challenges of the project at hand.

By improving the connection with others, it fosters constructive dialogue and prepares everyone, such that you achieve buy in whilst leaving your audience feeling bought into the process. There will be occasions when we need to showcase ideas and pitch forward points of interest, perhaps we need to set the scene, and draw powerful inferences. Pay attention to your opening lines and the gamut of what you are saying. There is nothing better than someone who sets the scene well and articulates with clarity, to grasp the audience's mind.

When time is not a constraint, you should be able to expand your opening gambit, setting the scene with precision, imagine sitting listening to someone and you have no idea what is about to be presented, you will sit there hesitant and unsure, apprehension then creeps in and our expressions will surely signal to the presented that something is amiss. In a face-to-face situation, take note of those expressions and body language signals which we emit, even though your words may be heard, your tone may throw you off course, or your expression may tell a completely different story. Your goal is to engage, to gently provoke, suggest, and guide your listeners to the message you wish to deliver. match your intonations with your subtle expressions of the hand, face, and body. In doing so, your words and expressions extend beyond your physical voice.

An important word expressed can be accompanied by a hand gesture, which subtly reinforces the message. Similarly, the rest of the points you develop should always remain flexible; able to be expanded, contracted, and rearranged to fit the circumstances at hand, it requires you to be present. As a rule of thumb: an engaged audience is always safer than one you have to continually try to second guess.

If part of your pitch mentions the value of collaboration, which is conceptual, relate that value in tangible terms: how precisely has collaboration helped you on a specific project with a specific issue. When outlining value, ensure there is an understanding of the underpinning construct of value and how it flows, the benefits and advantages which flow from it. Keep it simple!

Keep in mind that the best pitches are always succinct and to the point. Say everything you need to say, then stop. Don't beat your subject to death, and never bore your audience; use inflection points in your voice so that it resonates and expresses what you want to say. The second you bore your audience, you're finished. Strike out any habits which allow you to criticize, remove any form of innuendos and if there are any facets of ego present; they must go, as they have zero place when you are establishing relationships with others.

The best way to organize an effective pitch is to sketch it out, highlight the important aspects, if you're a visual person, use bubble maps to sequence the main points and corresponding points of interest. It's a great way of driving home the keywords you wish to articulate; by doing so, your audience will be able to connect the dots quickly. Get into a habit of remembering key words which make an impact and bring them alive with relevance.

Use conversational language. Avoid using buzz words to impress, state what needs to be stated. Look at the audience, and do not buckle if asked a question. If you don't know – don't fudge a response as your integrity will suffer. You are the facilitator, the conductor and as such can influence the mood of the audience, are they happy with a formal or casual tone, and to what extent they wish to be involved. You should never feel the need to confront when asked questions or use dialogue which comes across as rehearsed and scripted which loses natural rhythm.

Be prepared, to extend on matters of interest or indeed contention, think through how a long and short form of your pitch may unfold, set the scene, and reinforce those points of splendor with emphasis. Be sincere, and when asked a question, don't panic. If you don't know the answer, just say, "Let me come back to you on that." Don't fumble with weak responses; all that it will do is damage any good accomplished.

To hold your audience's attention, use frequent expressions of encouragement and back up bold statements with evidence, reinforce points of interest, and use tones which are engaging rather than sounding like a crashing bore, constantly speaking and using a monotonous tone will simply bore your audience, minds will wonder and boredom will set in.

Look for an opportunity to expand on the possible opportunities and benefits that you have to offer. Now that you have your audience's attention, provide a cohesive framing with the benefits and expected outcomes, seek inputs early, this way listeners will feel at ease and want to know more.

Don't overwhelm or frighten your audience; use gentle persuasion. Judge your audience carefully. Sometimes, you will need to take the lead; at other times, you will need to allow them plenty of room to make their own points. Ideally, any point they make will be based on what you have been saying to them; they will offer queries that demand more information. When you hear questions like "How does that work?" or "Tell me more," you know that you have caught their interest, and have a perfect opening to expand on your topic in detail. Pay attention to those tell-tale body language cues, if people are looking at away, this is a sign that they are disinterested. What you are seeking is a commitment to engage, share such that you feel they are glued to every word you say.

Find a way to strike a chord with your audience, to find common ground that will make any possible arrangement mutually beneficial. If circumstances allow, it is sometimes advantageous to bring other, well-established members of your network into the conversation which fuels the brainstorming process, by doing so, it reinforces your commitment to sharing and signposts everyone that you are open to ideas, and are willing to explore other possibilities.

During times of stressed disruptive dialogue, things can get out of hand, and we are faced with the age-old conundrum that has faced humans from the dawn of time: fight or flight kicks in. The term "fight or flight" describes a mechanism in the body that enables us to mobilize a lot of energy rapidly to cope with threats to survival. To understand the Fight or Flight response it helps to think about the role of emotions in our lives. Some of us prefer to focus on our logical, thinking nature and discount some of those colorful aspects of our emotions, which have a purpose.

Our most basic emotions like fear, anger or disgust are vital messengers: they evolved as signals to help us meet our basic needs for self-preservation and safety. The Fight or Flight response was designed to deal with feeling fear for our lives, but it is much more likely to be triggered by more complex and subtle concerns: internal threats in the form of worries. When we feel anxious or fearful about a presentation, perhaps an interview, a test, or social situation the Fight or Flight response is triggered in our body and we experience a range of strong, physical symptoms designed to temporarily change the way the body is functioning to enable a rapid physical response.

Make no mistake, when frustrations mount and solutions seem to recede into the distance, it can take a considerable effort to maintain communication in a positive, friendly manner. Frayed nerves and tired minds and bodies are more conducive to snapping and snipping than to a constructive exchange of ideas. When this happens, as it almost inevitably will at some point, it is the job of the leader to engage in conflict management and steer the proceedings back onto a positive track by finding a solution that will be acceptable to all parties involved.

One style does not fit all, how many styles do you have?

Chapter 21: The Value Of Conversation

Conversation is a creative process; we can use it establish new frontiers and build confidence in ourselves and others. It involves building avenues and frames of reference which are meaningful to all concerned. Sometimes we may express points of view or indeed over talk others, or dismiss extremely important facts of import. In such a case, all we are doing is placing unnecessary restrictions in the way of progress.

The ability to initiate and engage is an essential ingredient in the development of collaborative capabilities, both as a group and on a one-to-one level—through conversation we learn what makes people and teams tick and the approaches required to unlock the experiences and passions from within.

The skilled conversationalist to connect, virtually in person and through others. Effective conversations must go far beyond casual greetings, idle exchanges of pleasantries, and the relaying of instructions and dictates. Conversations can be many things: connection, communion, a search for the truth, a path to enlightened understanding, and can lead to an inner awakening.

Even casual conversation can make an idea suddenly click. it's like a conveyor belt, golden nuggets of information flow. At times, new angles illustrate previously unexplored potential. Great conversations provide momentum for previously unexplored concepts to be put in the spot light. Bad conversations are limited in value and lead to a trickle effect; with no lasting impressions made.

Think of how many great ideas emerge when we have a catch-up with colleagues around the informal areas at work, like the kitchen or huddle area, or in the corridor during an impromptu discussion. Think of those ah-ha moments which emerge from those casual interactions and discussions we have, and how entirely new perspectives, concepts, ideas generated provide better placed decisions and paths to follow.

We can't and shouldn't straight-jacket people into not expressing their views or sharing their ideas; working environments should be designed to help ideas be expressed, rather than to pigeonhole expression. At the heart of great conversations is communication, the nucleus of Innovation and change.

Hopefully, the leader will find allies who will help in the reconciliation process. When several parties collaborate to resolve a conflict, it is easier to encourage the rest of the group to openly express their concerns and work toward finding a mutually beneficial solution. The whole idea behind a collaboration is to find creative, non-confrontational ways to solve problems; this will inevitably lead to greater respect among members of the organization.

By addressing conflict rather than avoiding it, we build an understanding and transform tensions into possibilities. Think about the times when relationships have become strained because of a simple misunderstanding, something said in haste, an overreaction, aggressive tones, and innuendos. If only people's perspective could change in time to prevent situations from ever getting to this point, many projects would prosper instead of stalling and failing.

To facilitate communication, the leader must learn to exercise good listening skills. It is not enough to simply hear other people's words; it is essential that the leader listens as much to what is not being said as to what is. An extension of this ability is being able to analyze everyone's input and identify the main drivers of all parties.

Are you a great conversationalist?

Chapter 22: A Quick Guide

By understanding the distinctive hallmarks of synergy, we can learn how best to gauge and implement collaborative corporate strategies. This may demand an occasional quick check to determine where we are in a process. Below is an easy reference guide, which can be used in two different ways.

First, as a quick guide you can cross check where you are in the process, and chart areas which require review, and use it to train other team members on the important elements of the collaboration architecture to gain understanding and balance.

The second way to use it is to chart the areas you feel you are stuck on. This allows you explore, clarify and focus.

Step 1: Review points of interest

A. Focus on Relevance.

B. Develop the Scope and Intent.

Objective: Is to understand shared points of interest.

Why?

- To construct a broad outline of opportunities.

- Develop a better understanding of individual strengths.

- Define working culture and values alignment.

- Identify possible risks and discuss them.

- Assess areas which are weak or require greater synergy development.

Assess Initial Benefits of Collaboration

- What are the benefits which can accrue?

- How will you prioritize short, medium and long term benefits?

Drive Authenticity

- Are the relationship and intent real or just hype?

- Are you able to validate the commitments made?

- Can you see evidence through actions?

Strive for Momentum

- Is their balance in overall goals and dialogue?

- Are you to move from great ideas to real opportunities?

- Are team members able to resolve issues quickly and come to a common agreement?

In this phase, all actions are about evolving ideas to achieve greater clarity. It's the process which helps you power up, as if you are on the runway, about to take off. As we sit there the collaborative engines provide the thrust for lift off.

Step 2: Operate - Identify and Stimulate

Characterized by:

- A collective mission.

- Highly effective collaborative teams and relationships.

- Explore shared interests, opportunities, and challenges.

- Identify risks and assess how to mitigate them.

- Focus on priorities, quick-win actions, and those benefits that could flow right away. Agree on the top three focus areas, and why.

- Develop a common language around relevant areas which provide consistency across all participants.

- Ensure the checks and balances are in place.

- Determine evaluation methods and expectations.

Step 3: Sustain

- Cruising altitude - Begin to show the impact, share and ensure everyone sees the progress.

- Demonstrate that everyone can make a difference – ensure efficiency of effort.

- Develop back up plans, checks and balances.

- Continue to integrate different perspectives.

- Review evaluate and reflect findings, and renew or make corrective changes.

- Demonstrate sustainability and the qualify the impacts that are assumed.

Your options now are

1. Institutionalize, scale up, or find new angles to drive additional value.

Or

2. Continue with current efforts, exit, or wind down the collaboration.

Chapter 23: What Next?

As you reflect on ways to institute the methods, principles, and techniques laid out in the preceding pages of this book, it is essential that you begin looking for ways to consolidate your thinking and efforts. Some are obvious, easily identifiable, and relatively straightforward to deal with. Other areas may be more difficult, possibly even slightly uncomfortable—but they all require your attention if you are going to effectively unlock the power of collaborative leadership. To begin your journey toward greater collaborative abilities, ask yourself:

The greatest opportunities lie where?

A. What are the three top aspects you feel need development or changed, to enhance your collaborative capabilities?

B. How can you best derive value through collaboration?

C. What is the best way for you to leverage your core strengths?

An exercise you can do is imagine you are in an interview. What sort of questions could the interviewer ask, and how would you be able to demonstrate you understand collaboration? Are you able to talk about relationship management, collaboration and how you drive value?

In the end, what's next is entirely up to you. The tools inlaid in this text are as useful as any other: you can use them or set them aside. You can be part of the collective that drives yourself, your peers, your company, and the world, through to the next era of human development. No matter what you choose, you are going to apply your efforts somewhere.

By opening to collaboration in its truest sense, we can and will make a difference by leaving our own unique marks in the collective landscape of our world.

Now it's your turn. Make a list of the aspects that you feel define collaborative strengths.

1. What are the areas you feel need a further review?

2. What are the key drivers for collaboration?

3. Who are those individuals who inspire you?

What examples can you provide to support your claim that you truly are collaborative in nature?

- What are the trust enablers that underpin the projects or services that you offer?

- What might disrupt your level of trust and damage your progress?

- How could you co-create a different experience?

- What would specific areas of networking enhance your growth potential?

- What are the top three collaborative opportunities that would help you fast track growth?

- How socially intelligent are you?

- What is your collaborative elevator pitch?

- How would you define the economic or value exchange envisaged?

Are you clear on what your purpose is and what you need to do next to drive value for yourself and others?

If not turn back and establish something from this book which you can use to make a difference, thousands of others have!

Author's note on Robert Porter Lynch

To fill the gap in understanding and operating cooperative ventures, Mr. Lynch enjoys writing. He wrote the award-winning book, The Practical Guide to Joint Ventures and Corporate Alliances (John Wiley &Sons, 1987), which is based on his own experiences along with scores of other managers operating in the trenches. The architecture of cooperation is the focus of his best-selling book, Business Alliances: The Hidden Competitive Weapon, (John Wiley&Sons, 1993), which details the state-of-the-art in alliance formation, design, and operations. He wrote the popular chapter "Fostering Champions" for Peter Drucker's book The Leader of the Future (Jossey-Bass, 1997). His books have been translated into several languages, and his numerous articles on alliances have appeared in a broad range of magazines. He is often quoted in business journals such as Nation's Business, The Wall Street Journal, and The Conference Board Reports.

References

https://www.abraaj.com/insights/blogs/Op-ed-Arif-Naqvi-Reuters- forging- partnerships-creating-impact-a-new-model-for-business/

www.bsigroup.com/en-GB/Collaborative-Business-Relationships-ISO-44001/

https://www.burrus.com/2017/02/3-steps-build-strong-team/

www.ceospaceinternational.com/

www.chairmansnetwork.com

www.danielgoleman.info

www.drdaveinnovation.com

www.huckletree.com

www.iclinstitute.org/recources/publications

www.kilmanndiagnostics.com

www.oxigen.com

www.satalia.com

www.the-ggi.com

www.unipart.com